Mental Illness

Other Books of Related Interest:

Global Viewpoints Series

Health Care

Opposing Viewpoints Series

Eating Disorders

Health Care

Social Issues in Literature

Depression in Sylvia Plath's *The Bell Jar*

GLOBALVIEWPOINTS

Mental Illness

Noah Berlatsky, Book Editor

GREENHAVEN PRESS
A part of Gale, Cengage Learning

GALE
CENGAGE Learning·

Detroit • New York • San Francisco • New Haven, Conn • Waterville, Maine • London

Elizabeth Des Chenes, *Director, Publishing Solutions*

© 2013 Greenhaven Press, a part of Gale, Cengage Learning

Gale and Greenhaven Press are registered trademarks used herein under license.

For more information, contact:
Greenhaven Press
27500 Drake Rd.
Farmington Hills, MI 48331-3535
Or you can visit our Internet site at gale.cengage.com

For product information and technology assistance, contact us at

Gale Customer Support, 1-800-877-4253
For permission to use material from this text or product, submit all requests online at www.cengage.com/permissions

Further permissions questions can be emailed to permissionrequest@cengage.com

Articles in Greenhaven Press anthologies are often edited for length to meet page requirements. In addition, original titles of these works are changed to clearly present the main thesis and to explicitly indicate the author's opinion. Every effort is made to ensure that Greenhaven Press accurately reflects the original intent of the authors. Every effort has been made to trace the owners of copyrighted material.

Cover image © Peter Turnley/Corbis.

LIBRARY OF CONGRESS CATALOGING-IN-PUBLICATION DATA

Mental illness / Noah Berlatsky, book editor.
p. cm. -- (Global viewpoints)
Includes bibliographical references and index.
ISBN 978-0-7377-6268-6 (hbk.) -- ISBN 978-0-7377-6444-4 (pbk.)
1. Mental diseases. I. Berlatsky, Noah.
RC454.M392 2013
616.89--dc23

2012033590

Printed in Mexico
1 2 3 4 5 6 7 17 16 15 14 13

Contents

Foreword   11

Introduction   14

Chapter 1: Mental Illness and Trauma

1. **Afghanistan**'s Mental Health System Is   20
   Inadequate to Deal with the Stresses of War
   IRIN

   The ongoing war in Afghanistan has caused trauma and
   psychiatric distress to many Afghans. The country's mental health services are not sufficient to meet the
   population's needs.

2. **British** Soldiers Suffer from Post-Traumatic   26
   Stress After Serving in **Afghanistan**
   The Daily Mirror

   The number of British soldiers with post-traumatic stress
   disorder from serving in the war in Afghanistan is rising.
   More should be done to help them.

3. Worldwide, Holocaust Survivors and Their   33
   Children Suffer from Trauma
   Judy Siegel-Itzkovich

   Survivors living throughout the world continue to suffer
   from the traumatic effects of the Holocaust. Children
   and even grandchildren of survivors may also be affected.

4. **Haitians** Need Mental Health Services   40
   in the Wake of the 2010 Earthquake
   Julie R. Grier

   In January 2010, Haiti experienced a devastating earthquake. Haitians who lived through the quake are at increased risk of long-term mental health disorders. A targeted mental health response is needed.

5. **Japan** Needs to Respond Quickly and Effectively   53
   to Traumatic Stress Caused by Its Earthquake
   Metin Basoglu

Experts have claimed that mental health effects of earthquake disasters will not be that severe. This is not true. Therefore, survivors of the 2011 Japanese earthquake need to plan for long-term mental health care.

6. The Lingering Effects of Torture: Scientists   63
Assess the Long-Term Effects of Torture on the
Human Mind
Devin Powell

Psychological torture such as that used by US interrogators during the George W. Bush administration can have long-term psychological effects on victims.

Periodical and Internet Sources Bibliography   70

Chapter 2: Mental Illness and Human Rights

1. In **Israel**, as Worldwide, the Mentally Ill   72
Face Stigma and Discrimination
Amir Tal, David Roe, and Patrick W. Corrigan

In Israel, those with mental illness are stigmatized. Addressing social stigma is an important part of helping the mentally ill recover.

2. **Romania**'s Mentally Ill Are Treated   85
with Brutality and Contempt
Erich Wiedemann

Conditions in Romanian mental institutions are cruel and inhumane. The government refuses to make changes despite international pressure.

3. In the **United States**, Mentally Ill Prisoners   93
Face Inhumane Conditions
Human Rights Watch

The United States does not provide sufficient health services for mentally ill prisoners. In particular, it overuses solitary confinement, which can have serious mental health repercussions.

4. **Japan** Imposes the Death Penalty   107
on Mentally Ill Criminals
Amnesty International

Japan regularly executes prisoners who are mentally ill. This is a violation of human rights and should stop immediately.

5. In **China**, the Mental Health System Is Used   117
to Silence Political Dissent
Wan Yanhai

China has imprisoned in mental health facilities dissidents and opponents of the regime. At the same time, many people who are actually mentally ill cannot get help.

6. In **Russia**, the Mental Health System   124
May Be Used to Silence Political Dissent
Yuri Savenko, as told to Vaughan Bell

During the Soviet era, dissidents were often imprisoned in mental hospitals. There is some evidence that present-day Russia is again using mental health institutions for political purposes.

Periodical and Internet Sources Bibliography   131

Chapter 3: Mental Illness and Substance Abuse

1. Alcohol Use and Mental Health   133
in Developing Countries
Vikram Patel

Mental health issues in developing countries are serious. Alcoholism can also be a serious problem. More research is needed on the relationship between alcohol use and mental illness in these countries.

2. In **Ireland**, Alcohol Abuse Is Related to Mental   151
Illness and Suicide Among Young People
Alcohol Action Ireland

Suicide is a serious issue among young people in Ireland. Alcohol abuse, coupled with mental illness, can exacerbate this problem.

3. The Smoking Ban in the **United Kingdom**   158
Raises Difficult Issues for Mental Health Care
Professionals and Patients
Deborah Cornah

Because the mentally ill smoke at higher rates than the United Kingdom population as a whole, the 2007 ban on smoking in public places presents challenges to mental health professionals and patients.

4. To Address Substance Abuse and   168
   Mental Illness, **Southeast Asia** Needs to
   Shift to Community-Based Health Care
   Vijay Chandra
   Southeast Asia's mental health system has mostly been hospital based. The region needs to shift to a community-based health care system in treating mental illness.

5. **Eastern Europe** Has Unique Problems   175
   with Mental Illness and Substance Abuse
   Jane Salvage and Rob Keukens
   Eastern Europe's history and culture have influenced the relationship in the region between mental illness and substance abuse. Taking account of these factors can help point the way to improvements in treatment.

Periodical and Internet Sources Bibliography   187

Chapter 4: Mental Illness and Treatment

1. In **Singapore**, Treatment of Mental Illness   189
   Is Improving
   Siow-Ann Chong
   Treatment of mental illness in Singapore has been poor, in part because of the stigma attached to the mentally ill. Recently, however, treatment has been improving.

2. In **Canada**, Providing the Mentally Ill   196
   with Housing Can Aid Them in Recovery
   Canadian Mental Health Association (Ontario)
   Canadian programs that provide the mentally ill with stable housing have been successful in promoting recovery.

3. In **South Africa**, Mental Health Treatment   206
   Should Be Incorporated into Care for HIV/AIDS
   Khopotso Bodibe

People who suffer from HIV also have high rates of mental illness, partially due to the disease and partially due to stress. Mental health care should be a part of caring for HIV/AIDS patients in South Africa.

4. In **Argentina**, a Treatment Program   212
   Providing Companionship for the Mentally Ill
   Has Been Successful
   Marcela Valente

   In Argentina, a program provides paid companions to people released from psychiatric care. The program has helped prevent relapse among patients and has also provided employment for jobless people.

5. **Mexico** Needs to Improve Its Treatment   218
   of Mental Illness in Adolescents
   G. Borges, C. Benjet, ME Medina-Mora,
   R. Orozco, and PS Wang

   Mentally ill adolescents in Mexico urgently need better mental health services. More resources and reallocation of resources are desperately needed.

Periodical and Internet Sources Bibliography   225

For Further Discussion   226

Organizations to Contact   228

Bibliography of Books   233

Index   236

Foreword

"The problems of all of humanity can
only be solved by all of humanity."
—Swiss author Friedrich Dürrenmatt

Global interdependence has become an undeniable reality. Mass media and technology have increased worldwide access to information and created a society of global citizens. Understanding and navigating this global community is a challenge, requiring a high degree of information literacy and a new level of learning sophistication.

Building on the success of its flagship series, Opposing Viewpoints, Greenhaven Press has created the Global Viewpoints series to examine a broad range of current, often controversial topics of worldwide importance from a variety of international perspectives. Providing students and other readers with the information they need to explore global connections and think critically about worldwide implications, each Global Viewpoints volume offers a panoramic view of a topic of widespread significance.

Drugs, famine, immigration—a broad, international treatment is essential to do justice to social, environmental, health, and political issues such as these. Junior high, high school, and early college students, as well as general readers, can all use Global Viewpoints anthologies to discern the complexities relating to each issue. Readers will be able to examine unique national perspectives while, at the same time, appreciating the interconnectedness that global priorities bring to all nations and cultures.

Material in each volume is selected from a diverse range of sources, including journals, magazines, newspapers, nonfiction books, speeches, government documents, pamphlets, organization newsletters, and position papers. Global Viewpoints is truly global, with material drawn primarily from international sources available in English and secondarily from US sources with extensive international coverage.

Features of each volume in the Global Viewpoints series include:

- An **annotated table of contents** that provides a brief summary of each essay in the volume, including the name of the country or area covered in the essay.

- An **introduction** specific to the volume topic.

- A **world map** to help readers locate the countries or areas covered in the essays.

- For each viewpoint, an **introduction** that contains notes about the author and source of the viewpoint explains why material from the specific country is being presented, summarizes the main points of the viewpoint, and offers three **guided reading questions** to aid in understanding and comprehension.

- **For further discussion** questions that promote critical thinking by asking the reader to compare and contrast aspects of the viewpoints or draw conclusions about perspectives and arguments.

- A worldwide list of **organizations to contact** for readers seeking additional information.

- A **periodical bibliography** for each chapter and a **bibliography of books** on the volume topic to aid in further research.

- A comprehensive **subject index** to offer access to people, places, events, and subjects cited in the text, with the countries covered in the viewpoints highlighted.

Global Viewpoints is designed for a broad spectrum of readers who want to learn more about current events, history, political science, government, international relations, economics, environmental science, world cultures, and sociology—students doing research for class assignments or debates, teachers and faculty seeking to supplement course materials, and others wanting to understand current issues better. By presenting how people in various countries perceive the root causes, current consequences, and proposed solutions to worldwide challenges, Global Viewpoints volumes offer readers opportunities to enhance their global awareness and their knowledge of cultures worldwide.

Introduction

> *"Women from a biological point of view are different than men, and worldwide they suffer from more discrimination and violence, which are risk factors for mental illness such as depression."*
>
> —International
> Association for Women's
> Mental Health, 4th World Congress
> on Women's Mental Health, 2011

Worldwide, women have specific challenges when it comes to mental illness. The World Health Organization (WHO) in an article on its website notes that whether an individual is a man or a woman is a "critical determinant" of mental health and of the kind of care and treatment the individual will receive.

In particular, according to WHO, women are much more likely to suffer from depression than are men. In part, WHO says, this discrepancy may be due to the bias of medical professionals; because of preconceptions about gender, doctors are simply more likely to diagnose women with depression. However, WHO says, the high rates of depression among women are also due to the fact that women suffer from "gender-based violence, socioeconomic disadvantage, low income and income inequality . . . and unremitting responsibility for the care of others." In other words, women worldwide are the victims of sexism, which can be a major cause of stress, anxiety, and even (in the case of sexual violence) trauma. In fact, WHO says that women are the "largest single group of people" suffering from post-traumatic stress disorder.

There are numerous studies worldwide that have provided support for WHO's suggestion that mental illness among women is frequently linked to gender violence. For example, in a June 26, 2009, article on AllAfrica.com, Ama Achiaa Amankwah reports that women in Ghana who were raped as children had a 30 percent greater risk of developing mental illness than women who were not raped.

Similarly, a February 2008 article by AB Ludermir et al. in *Social Science and Medicine* surveyed women in Brazil to try to track the relationship between domestic violence and common mental disorders such as anxiety and depression. The researchers found that "the prevalence of mental disorders was 49.0% among women who reported any type of violence and 19.6% among those who did not report violence." The authors of the report therefore concluded that to reduce mental illness among women, Brazil must implement policies aimed at reducing domestic violence.

In some cases, gender and cultural norms can interact in ways that make it difficult for women to seek help for mental illnesses. In the United States, for example, Asian American women "have the highest suicide rates among American females in the 15–24 age group," while Asian American women over sixty-five have ten times the suicide rate of other women in their age group, according to an August 11, 2008, article by Tina Peng in *Newsweek*.

The high levels of mental illness among Asian American women are in part the result of stigma in Asian communities that links mental illness to personal weakness. In addition to such factors, Asian American women in particular are often under great cultural pressure to be "perfect daughters, wives, mothers, and nurturers, always putting others before themselves," according to an October 2009 article on the website of the National Alliance on Mental Illness. Thus, traditional expectations and stereotypes of women can contribute to stress and prevent women from treating mental illness.

In the Arab world, the inequality of women can create widespread mental health difficulties. In a September 2007 paper in the *Journal of Affective Disorders*, S. Douki et al. report that in Arab communities, women have a higher prevalence of depression, eating disorders, and suicidal behavior. In addition, the authors say, women in these communities "are more stigmatized, have less access to care and suffer from a worse social outcome." The authors conclude that to address the mental health of women, caregivers need to address the social and cultural context that stigmatizes and subordinates women. In other words, women need more rights and more equality if they are to have better mental health outcomes.

According to Zofeen Ebrahim in a February 1, 2010, article for the Inter Press Service news agency, inequality in Pakistan can also lead to mental illness among women in that country. However, Ebrahim argues, while mental illness is a real problem for many women, diagnoses of mental illness are also used as a way to incarcerate women who do not conform to Pakistani society's expectations. Women who refuse to marry, seek a divorce, or resist domestic violence may be "simply labeled as 'mentally ill' in order to avoid the threat to family honour," according to Pakistani clinical psychologist Dr. Asha Bedar. Thus, mental health facilities can become a way to enforce gender inequality rather than a way to help women.

There are also some situations in which being male appears to put men at greater mental health risk. For example, WHO says that worldwide men are much more likely to suffer from alcoholism than are women. Similarly, a European Union report, "Mental Health in Europe: A Gender Perspective," found that women were more likely than men to seek help for a mental illness when they were in distress.

In China, sexism has contradictorily resulted in some serious health consequences for men. China state policy has long limited families to one child in an effort to reduce the population. However, Chinese families have traditionally had a strong cultural preference for sons. As a result, many parents, in an effort to make sure their one allowed child is a boy rather than a girl, have chosen to abort female children. Thus, there is a sizable demographic dearth of women in China. This "shortage of women may have increased mental health problems and socially disruptive behavior among men and has left some men unable to marry and have a family," according to a September 15, 2005, article by Therese Hesketh and Wei-Xing Zhu in the *New England Journal of Medicine*.

This volume examines other mental health issues in chapters focusing on mental illness and trauma, mental illness and human rights, mental illness and substance abuse, and mental illness and treatment. Different writers offer various perspectives on how mental illnesses are recognized and treated around the world.

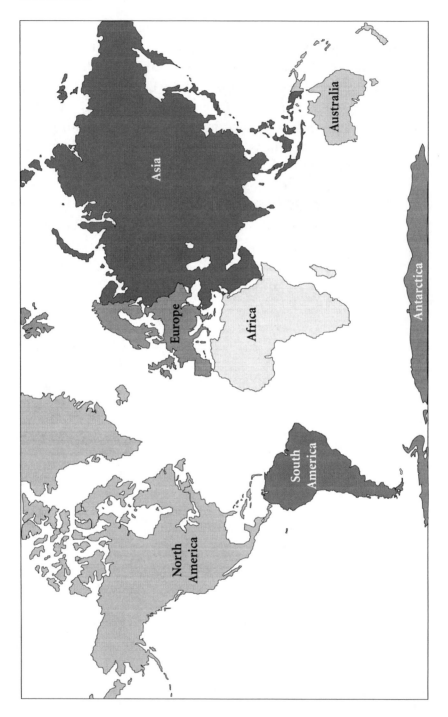

CHAPTER 1

Mental Illness and Trauma

Afghanistan's Mental Health System Is Inadequate to Deal with the Stresses of War

IRIN

IRIN, or the Integrated Regional Information Networks, is a project of the United Nations Office for the Coordination of Humanitarian Affairs, and it reports on humanitarian issues worldwide. In the following viewpoint, IRIN claims that there is a high rate of mental illness and trauma among Afghans. IRIN says this phenomenon is related to the ongoing war in Afghanistan as well as to issues such as domestic violence and extreme poverty. IRIN asserts that Afghanistan has only very limited resources to treat the mentally ill, resulting in a crisis of care. According to the author, Afghani health officials are attempting to improve mental health services.

As you read, consider the following questions:

1. What percentage of Afghans suffer from stress disorders and mental problems, according to the Ministry of Public Health?

2. What did the *Journal of the American Medical Association* report as a common trauma event in Afghanistan?

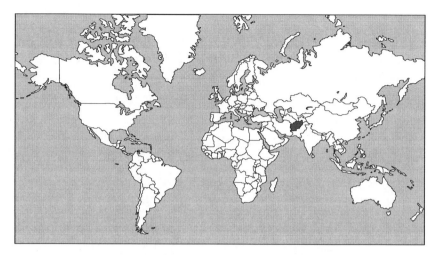

3. According to a hospital specialist, how much money for medicines does the mental health hospital in Kabul receive monthly? How much is that per patient?

He sleeps in derelict outbuildings, eats dirty leftovers, wears tattered clothes and spends his days on the streets. He knows neither his name, nor his age, nor any relatives. People give him a wide berth despite—or because of—his frantic begging gestures. He is middle-aged and mentally ill in Kabul city.

Multiple Causes

At least one in 10 of the over 700 street beggars arrested in Kabul in the past 10 months [through October 2009] have mental disorders of some kind, according to officials in the government's anti-begging commission.

"We cannot keep these people because we have no resources, so we just let them go," Nowroz Ali Alizada, an official of the Afghan Red Crescent Society (ARCS) and a member of the anti-begging commission, told IRIN [the Integrated Regional Information Networks].

ARCS has sheltered 130 people suffering from psychosis in Kabul and Herat provinces but says it cannot take care of other equally needy and abandoned patients.

It is unclear how many Afghans suffer from severe types of mental and psychiatric disorders but surveys conducted by NGOs [nongovernmental organizations], such as Care International and Physicians for Human Rights, have shown a high prevalence of post-traumatic stress disorder (PTSD), manic depression and anxiety among Afghans.

"Recent surveys conducted by national and international organizations indicate that 66 percent of [all] Afghans are suffering from stress disorders and mental problems," the Ministry of Public Health (MoPH) said in a statement on 11 October [2009].

"War and physical violence has caused general damage to the mental health of many Afghans," said Musadiq Nadimee, a psychiatrist at Kabul's mental health hospital (MHH). [Editor's note: Afghanistan has been at war since a US-led force invaded the country in 2001.]

Surveys conducted by NGOs ... have shown a high prevalence of post-traumatic stress disorder (PTSD), manic depression and anxiety among Afghans.

However, the causes of mental illness are not confined to acts of war, experts say.

Domestic violence, extreme poverty and lack of access to treatment and rehabilitation services are some of the drivers of mental illnesses.

According to a report entitled "Violence, Suffering, and Mental Health in Afghanistan: A School-Based Survey" by the UK [United Kingdom] medical journal the *Lancet*: "In Afghanistan, there is a spectrum of violence—ranging from armed insurgency to family conflict—which generates sudden pain and persistent suffering. Our data suggest that, in Afghan children's lives, everyday violence matters just as much as militarized violence in the recollection of traumatic experiences.

"Some children identified severe domestic beatings, a severe accident, or a frightening medical treatment as more traumatic than having witnessed parents and grandparents being killed in rocket attacks," the report said.

While mental health disorders appear to be rife, there is only one psychiatric hospital serving a population of 27–28 million.

Lack of access to food and water was reported as a common trauma event experienced by over 56 percent of the non-disabled persons interviewed for a study in the *Journal of the American Medical Association* in 2004. Lack of shelter was reported as a main trauma event for about 70 percent of the disabled respondents of the same survey.

No Voice

While mental disorders appear to be rife, there is only one psychiatric hospital serving a population of 27–28 million. About 80–100 patients are attending the 60-bed MHH in Kabul.

Health workers in the MHH, who requested anonymity, told IRIN about some of the problems.

"We receive only the equivalent of US$100 monthly for medicines for over 2,500 patients [four US cents per patient]," said a specialist at the hospital.

"Patients and their carers often stand in queues in front of the only toilet in the hospital," said another psychiatrist. "The main problem is that people suffering from psychosis and mental illness cannot air their problems so it's like a 'nothing heard nothing happens' situation."

Women and Mental Health in Afghanistan

Over two million Afghans suffer from levels of stress disorder due to the long period of conflict, according to the estimates in the Country Cooperation Strategy report. Affected is the capacity of the health care system to respond to the mental health needs. Mental health has not been addressed in the past decades and little is known about patterns of mental illness. In prewar time [before the 2001 U.S.-led invasion], studies indicate that Afghanistan's mental health was not that different from other developing countries. During the [strict fundamentalist Islamic preinvasion] Taliban regime, high percentages of women living in the Taliban-controlled area compared with non-Taliban areas suffered from major depression, 78 to 28 percent respectively; and from suicidal ideation, 65 to 18 percent respectively. Another study found that 42 percent of women suffered post-traumatic stress, 97 percent experienced depression and 86 percent had anxiety.

The high rates of mental problems may be related to Taliban policies of gender segregation and denial of basic human rights to women. Further the report states, "The fall of the Taliban regime, however, has not resulted in an improvement in the mental health status of the population." A nationwide survey conducted in the first year after the U.S.-led invasion found high levels of depression symptoms (male: 59.1 percent, female: 73.4 percent), anxiety symptoms (male 59.3 percent, female 83.5 percent) and post-traumatic stress disorder (male 32.1 percent, female 48.3 percent).

Rosemarie Skaine,
Women of Afghanistan in the Post-Taliban Era:
How Lives Have Changed and Where They Stand Today,
Jefferson, NC: McFarland & Company, 2008, p. 117.

Officials at MoPH said efforts were under way to attract more donor funding and garner other resources to boost mental health services. They said a national mental health strategy had been finalized, a mental health task force had been established in the MoPH, and 16 psycho-social centres had been established in Kabul and Herat provinces.

"In the near future MoPH will ensure that at least one trained mental health professional is working in every health facility and that every patient has the opportunity to be screened and get proper counselling and treatment for mental health and psycho-social problems," said [Sayed] Mohammad Amin Fatimie, the minister of public health.

British Soldiers Suffer from Post-Traumatic Stress After Serving in Afghanistan

The Daily Mirror

The Daily Mirror *is a British newspaper. In the following viewpoint, the author reports on the experience of post-traumatic stress disorder among British soldiers who have served in the wars in Afghanistan and Iraq. The* Daily Mirror *says that the number of troops and ex-service members with mental health problems is increasing. The author reports on several veterans who have committed suicide apparently because of trauma suffered during their service. The veterans' mothers blame their sons' suicides on the failure of the government to provide health care and help. The* Daily Mirror *argues that more needs to be done to help British veterans traumatized by violence in Afghanistan and other wars.*

As you read, consider the following questions:

1. What statistics does the viewpoint cite to show that mental illness among veterans increased between 2007 and 2010?

2. According to an MoD spokesman, why has there been a rise in reports of PTSD among veterans?

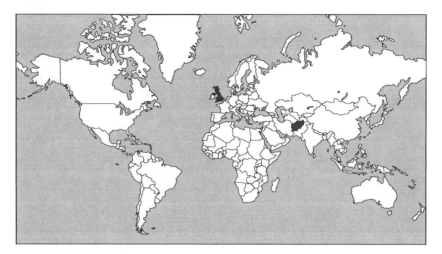

3. Why did June Black and Nicola Howat become close friends, according to the viewpoint?

They are the wounds that cannot be seen—but they can be just as devastating and often harder to treat.

PTSD Is Worsening

And the problem of British troops mentally scarred by their experiences in Afghanistan and Iraq is getting dramatically worse.[1]

A *Mirror* investigation has found a significant increase in the number of our service personnel being treated for mental health issues, including post-traumatic stress disorder [PTSD].

Between 2007 and 2010, the total with mental health problems soared from 2,289 to 2,510—a 9.7% increase. And those diagnosed with severe PTSD leaped from 122 in 2007 to 185 in 2010—a 51% rise.

The shocking statistics cover all ranks, from top brass to privates. The army currently has around 100,000 troops—with 9,500 of them serving in Afghanistan.

1. British soldiers were part of the coalition that invaded Afghanistan in 2001, and part of the coalition that invaded Iraq in 2003.

Figures obtained under freedom of information laws reveal that 9,064 soldiers and officers had some type of mental disorder between January 1, 2007, and December 31, 2010.

They included those suffering anxiety and mood swings—as well as 509 confirmed cases of post-traumatic stress disorder.

Some 2,510 troops were diagnosed with mental problems in 2010, the most recent figures available. A total of 185 of these cases were later identified as PTSD.

Frontline soldiers suffer most. In 2010, 1,157 privates were diagnosed with mental illness, with around 10% of the cases found to be PTSD.

Psychotherapist and retired army colonel Tony Gauvain is an expert in the treatment of military PTSD. He said: "A generation has been blighted. This is a ticking time bomb.

"The tightness of the PTSD definition allows the MoD [Ministry of Defence] to minimise its liability, but it's highly significant that they do refer to mental health disorders.

"PTSD is actually an umbrella term which covers numerous things such as depression, anxiety, self-medication and other symptoms.

"This is the tip of the iceberg. We are dealing with people who served in the Falklands [referring to a conflict fought between Britain and Argentina in 1982] 30 years ago and there would have been soldiers from World War One who were still having nightmares years down the line."

"A generation has been blighted. This [mental illness] is a ticking time bomb."

In 1982 during the two-month Falklands conflict, 255 British troops were killed.

But that figure has been eclipsed by the number who have since committed suicide—currently around 300, according to the South Atlantic Medal Association.

A Coiled Spring

Col Gauvain, chair of charity PTSD Resolution, said: "It is a massive problem that is likely to get worse. Sometimes the traumatic memory of combat can lay dormant, like a coiled spring, and it just takes a small event to push someone over the edge."

Former SAS [Special Air Service] commander Colonel Clive Fairweather said: "All wars produce mental as well as physical casualties.

"There is still a lot of stigma surrounding mental illness, but the earlier people come forward, the easier it can be to treat."

"Sometimes the traumatic memory of combat can lay dormant, like a coiled spring, and it just takes a small event to push someone over the edge."

Charities including Combat Stress and Help for Heroes, who deal with personnel from the Falklands, 1991 Gulf War, Northern Ireland, the Balkans and Sierra Leone [all wars in which British troops fought], are being approached by an increasing number of veterans seeking help.

Last year [2011] Combat Stress received 1443 referrals—10% up on 2010.

An MoD spokesman said the rise was triggered by soldiers being more willing to come forward to discuss their problems. He added: "The mental well-being of service personnel is a priority."

Soldier Suicides

Two military mums united in grief after their sons committed suicide have said more must be done to help troops readjust to civilian life.

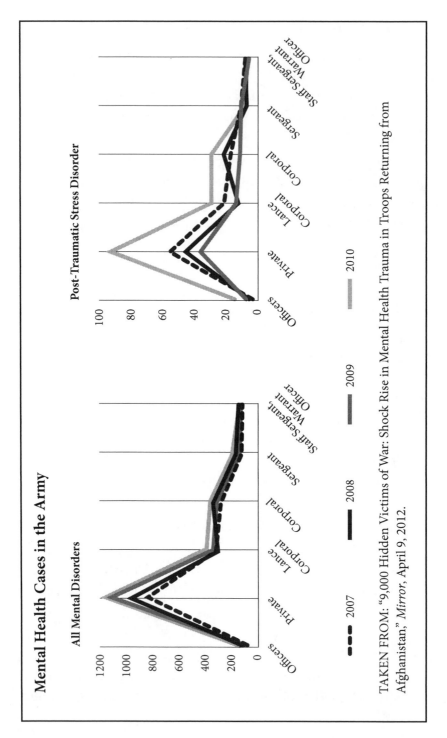

Mental Health Cases in the Army

All Mental Disorders

Post-Traumatic Stress Disorder

TAKEN FROM: "9,000 Hidden Victims of War: Shock Rise in Mental Health Trauma in Troops Returning from Afghanistan," *Mirror*, April 9, 2012.

June Black, 54, and Nicola Howat, 40, have become close friends after their boys hanged themselves within weeks of each other after their tours ended.

Private Aaron Black and Private James Lindsay, both 22, served with 3 Scots, the Black Watch [an infantry battalion], during one of the most mentally demanding deployments in Afghanistan's Helmand Province of recent years.

Pte Black, of Blairgowrie, Perthshire, was found hanged on December 17 after laying out a photo of himself in his uniform beside his two medals and a picture of an ex-girlfriend.

Mum June said: "I just got a text from him saying 'Goodbye XXX'. There is support there for the soldiers but they have to go looking for it.

"When he came back from Afghanistan, he could be quite jumpy. It was horrible. You can't imagine what he saw and went through."

She added: "There should be a follow-up process for young service leavers from the army.

"It may have made a difference if a charity or group had checked with him after a month and perhaps at regular intervals to see if he was coping."

Five weeks after Aaron's death, Pte Lindsay—who served in the army for nearly four years—took his life in similar circumstances.

Mum Nicola, from Lincluden, Dumfries, said: "He didn't talk much about what went on there.

"He did once tell me about having to put body parts into wee bags after a soldier was blown up.

"I could hear him screaming at night. Sometimes he seemed all right but then he'd just fly off the handle."

Nicola added: "It was definitely his experiences that caused him to take his life.

"More should be done to help soldiers adjust. It's sickening.

"He was going to counselling but he just had something in his head that he struggled with."

Worldwide, Holocaust Survivors and Their Children Suffer from Trauma

Judy Siegel-Itzkovich

Judy Siegel-Itzkovich is the health and sciences editor at the Jerusalem Post. In the following viewpoint, she discusses the work of Natan Kellermann, who has researched the effects of trauma on Holocaust victims and their descendants. Kellermann argues that the children of many Holocaust survivors suffer from trauma and anxiety caused by their parents' experiences. Kellermann is himself the child of a survivor, and Siegel-Itzkovich reports on some of the effects of the trauma on Kellermann's life. Kellermann also suggests that even the grandchildren of survivors may experience some effects of trauma.

As you read, consider the following questions:

1. Why does Yehuda Bauer argue that the Holocaust was unlike any other genocide in history?
2. What assumptions about Holocaust survivors have been accepted at various times, according to Siegel-Itzkovich?
3. Why do some researchers believe that the offspring of survivors who were small orphans at liberation had unique problems, according to Kellermann?

Holocaust survivors bear emotional scars that are not easily healed. Research has also shown that many children of survivors—raised by traumatized parents—tend to be different than peers who had no connection to the Shoah [the Holocaust]. But an Israeli clinical psychologist (and son of survivors) who "grew up in a country far removed from the horrors of the Holocaust" says that the grandchildren of survivors may also be touched by the unspeakable horrors.

The Survivors' Experiences

Dr. Natan Kellermann, who has worked with survivors and their families for over a decade, recently wrote a new English-language book called *Holocaust Trauma: Psychological Effects and Treatment*. Published by www.iuniverse.com, the academic soft cover is based on his own research and that of others. Of the 206 pages, almost 40 consist of references to studies.

The author, who was born in Sweden where his parents moved after the Shoah, is currently project development director of the National Israeli Center for Psychological Support of Survivors of the Holocaust and the Second Generation (Amcha)—which likely will go on to counsel the third generation when the ageing survivors are gone. Kellermann focuses on Israeli survivors. However, he devotes chapters to Jewish survivors and their descendants abroad as well as to the collective effects on the populations of Germany, Austria and other European countries whose relatives took an active part in the mass murder.

Amcha president Prof. Haim Dasberg writes in the foreword that "Holocaust survivors living among us were part of the conspiracy of silence for many years. They attempted to be like other Israelis, living through the developmental phase of a Jewish national consciousness. Until the 1980s, it was not a particular honor to be a Holocaust survivor, except for the few ghetto fighters who founded the kibbutzim Yad Mordechai and Lohamei Haghettaot and who held seats in parliament." But, Dasberg continues, "denial of being a Holocaust survivor was a psychological necessity for coping, and indeed Holocaust survivors thrive in society." After the phase of denial came the phase of ambivalence and doubt, occurring mainly around the years between the Yom Kippur War [1973] and the first Gulf War [1991]. During those years, a "general empathy and identification with the survivors began." The Amcha president said the motto for Kellermann's book is: "Remember the past and live in the present," but he adds that the future is also important, and wishes success for the therapists who took on the burden of working with survivors and their descendants.

The Second Generation

In his preface, after quoting [author] William Faulkner who said "The past is not dead. In fact, it's not even past," Kellermann describes his own experience as a member of the second generation. His mother, Lily, was at 15 given the number A8816 in the Auschwitz-Birkenau death camp. She was selected for work while her parents and younger siblings were gassed. A year later, barely alive, she was liberated by the British on April 15, 1945, and sent to Sweden for rehabilitation for five years. She met her husband and gave birth to two sons, with Natan being the younger. "Even though I was born and grew up in a country far removed from the horrors of the Holocaust, I have lived with its images for my entire life," he writes.

Scenes that seem like fiction to those who are not survivors or their descendants are alive for people like survivors and [Natan Kellermann].

His mother, who was fully functioning and loving, told him very little about her traumatic experiences, but her Holocaust trauma "has painfully permeated my inner life. . . . Gruesome Holocaust associations fill my waking and sleeping life, and human suffering is a constant companion. As have so many other children of survivors, I have apparently absorbed some of the psychological burdens of my parents and share their grief and terror. It is no coincidence that I became a psychologist and a psycho-dramatist, and that much of my professional interest has focused on individual and collective trauma," he confesses.

He goes on to say that scenes that seem like fiction to those who are not survivors or their descendants are alive for people like survivors and himself. ". . . We imagine a father holding his child in his arms and watching it starve to death, without having any food to give it; we imagine the child lying next to his mother, searching for warmth, only to realize that she has frozen to death. We imagine the death anxiety of all those who knew they were about to be shot, or hanged, or buried, or gassed or whatever other method of murder was about to be enacted upon them. We imagine the heartbreaking separations between family members in which mothers gave away their babies in order to choose life."

But the psychologist doesn't focus on himself; besides reporting on scores of scientific studies, he also presents the personal stories of a number of survivors and second- and third-generation descendants who described their feelings and experiences in workshops. He recalled one survivor who told her tearful granddaughter: "No, no, no. We did not pass on any of our trauma to you, and you do not need to be upset."

While Kellermann concedes that there have been other major human catastrophes and even genocides, he cites Yad Vashem scholar Prof. Yehuda Bauer who said there "is still no other genocide that compares to the Holocaust, neither in its intensity of evil nor in the pain of individuals made to suffer precisely because they were a specific group of people, not in the ghastly scope of its cruel ambitions, not in the combination of twisted ideas and wicked actions that, for a time, threatened to engulf our entire world. The Holocaust was unique in its scope, magnitude and methodology. It was the most systematic, merciless and effective mass murder in human history, a disaster of enormous proportions that we are only now beginning to grasp. This fact is what makes this event so much more malignant than many of the other genocides."

Theories About Survivors' Mental Health

The Amcha psychologist notes that professionals in the field had gradually accepted a number of assumptions—one replacing the other—about Holocaust survivors. The first was that survivors who showed signs of severe mental distress after the war suffered from some kind of mental problem before the war. Next came the view that some survivors who had been healthy before the Holocaust became mentally ill from their war experiences. Then, they supposed that instead of traumatized survivors improving, some conditions became worse as the years went by.

It is clear that survivors should be treated for the problems and pain they have.

Some professionals who thought survivors who were healthy before the war and functioned adequately after 1945 could develop late effects as a result of anxiety-provoking associations, a new trauma or simply old age. But most recently, a new view emerged that regarded survivors as being healthy before the war and that a majority had recuperated well afterwards due to their natural resilience. Most survivors have never been diagnosed with a mental illness, these professionals argue, nor did they require psychiatric treatment. Yet another view suggested a more complex picture, in which many survivors did suffer from post-traumatic stress disorder (PTSD) but nevertheless succeeded in adjusting to peace-time life.

Finally, wrote Kellermann, psychologists are now trying to integrate all the previous assumptions, even though some are contradictory. So survivors are both vulnerable and resistant, suffered severe traumatization and extraordinary growth, and had severe periods of emotional suffering and symptoms plus emotional balance and creativity. In any case, it is clear that survivors should be treated for the problems and pain they have. Kellermann explains how the problems of survivors who were small children during the Holocaust clearly had different problems than those who were already adults.

An interesting chapter is devoted to Holocaust trauma in the children of survivors. It begins with a quote from Siegi Hirsch, an Auschwitz survivor: "For a long time, I recounted to my children that the six-digit number tattooed on my forearm was the telephone number of an old friend."

Survivors may be able to relate experiences to their grandchildren that they were ashamed to tell their own children.

The Trauma Runs Deep

Kellermann has encountered many of the second generation who suffer from nightmares as if they had experienced traumatic events themselves. However, the way this trauma is transmitted is very complex, he writes. Some in the second generation feel they have to be super-achievers to be living replacements for those murdered in the Holocaust, he says. One woman whose parents survived confessed that she still has problems buying her children clothing with vertical stripes, as she saw a photo of her father in his camp uniform. When another member of the second generation was told by her dentist that she should have her wisdom tooth extracted, she was shocked as she thought of corpses whose gold teeth were removed by order of the Nazis. Some children of survivors have problems with interpersonal relations, or fear shortages of things and want a spare of everything. Some survivors have caused problems by being overbearing, and too involved in their grown-up children's lives.

Kellermann notes that some researchers believe the offspring of survivors who were small orphans at liberation had unique problems because their parents did not have models for family life and have trouble showing affection to their spouses and children.

The grandchildren of survivors may also carry the baggage of the Holocaust. The extent of trauma in this generation is not well studied, but they may also provide opportunities for survivors to discuss their lives in a calmer way, and their stories could produce strong emotional ties with the youngest generation; survivors may be able to relate experiences to their grandchildren that they were ashamed to tell their own children, the author writes.

Kellermann concludes with his deep discomfort from viewing scenes in which Israelis are called "Nazis" by demonstrators in Europe and elsewhere, and his frustration over the world's misunderstanding.

Haitians Need Mental Health Services in the Wake of the 2010 Earthquake

Julie R. Grier

Julie R. Grier is a mental health specialist and an independent researcher at Maastricht University who has been working on mental health issues in Haiti since 2008. In the following viewpoint, she argues that the Haitian earthquake of 2010 will have serious mental health consequences for the Haitians who experienced it. She argues that a coordinated mental health response must be put in place. She says that this response should be most intense in the first eighteen months after the disaster, but that it should be designed to continue indefinitely after that, since it will take an extended period of time for Haiti to rebuild.

As you read, consider the following questions:

1. According to Grier, what pre-exposure factors in place before a traumatic event may influence the degree of psychiatric distress that a victim suffers?
2. What does Grier say is the general attitude toward mental illness in Haiti, and how are people with emotional disturbances perceived?

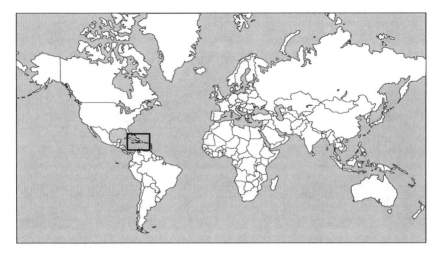

3. Why does Grier say that it is important for mental health professionals to reach out to religious leaders?

On 12 January 2010, Port-au-Prince and much of southern Haiti were decimated by a powerful earthquake (magnitude 7.0). Hundreds of thousands are now confirmed dead and the millions of victims who survived are facing homelessness, grief, and inadequate food, water, and health care. The physical devastation in the wake of this event is enormous and obvious; the emotional damage is similar in size, but far less visible.

As survivors of a large disaster, the Haitian population in the affected regions are now at increased risk of developing long-term mental health disorders, including depression, anxiety, post-traumatic stress disorder, and substance abuse. All of these illnesses can be debilitating, decreasing the productivity potential of people suffering from them, and they can include psychosomatic symptoms, physical complaints of emotional origin that will lead people to seek out physical medical assistance at a time when health infrastructure is already overwhelmed. The long-term impact of trauma-related mental health disorders in individuals can be severely negative; the implications this carries when an entire society has experienced trauma cannot be ignored. A targeted mental health response is clearly needed, including evaluation, near-term intervention, long-term intervention, and preparing the community for future disasters.

What Is Trauma and Why Does It Matter?

Traumatic stressors include all incidents outside of the usual range of situations a person deals with and they all involve experiencing intense fear for one's own safety or that of a loved one. Although life for most Haitians prior to the earthquake was characterized by deep poverty, food insecurity, and political instability, the earthquake itself was far beyond the usual range of situations even these put-upon people encountered. Survivors now live in a constant state of intense fear for their own safety and that of loved ones, particularly since the region continues to experience large aftershocks. Adding to the stress, food and health care are in short supply, increasing the likelihood of deaths caused by malnutrition, opportunistic infection, and disease generally. Essentially, survivors of the quake have experienced the significant trauma of the quake itself and continue to experience the traumatic stressor of life in a third-world disaster area.

A wide range of disorders have been found in populations following exposure to a traumatic event. These include strictly emotional or mental disorders such as post-traumatic stress disorder (PTSD), depression, and generalized anxiety disorder (GAD); organic, physical disorders resulting from injury that inhibit the victim's cognitive functioning; and psychically linked somatic complaints and physiological disruptions or alterations affecting the brain and nervous system.

Trauma victims are also at increased risk for substance abuse, early death, and suicide. These disorders inhibit the social and occupational (i.e., economic) capacity of the people suffering from them, thereby making the challenge of reconstructing or reinforcing southern Haiti's crumpled social, economic, and political institutions even more daunting than if the victims and responding policy makers were facing only physical effects of the earthquake.

Survivors of the quake have experienced the significant trauma of the quake itself and continue to experience the traumatic stressor of life in a third-world disaster area.

Not everyone who experiences a traumatic event will develop a full-blown trauma-related illness. However, acute stress disorder, a short-term anxiety disorder consisting of "abnormal behavior that interferes with survival" in times of crisis or danger (such as the situation in Haiti at this moment), can occur in the vast majority (as high as 80%) of people exposed to a stressor. It has been further found that if these symptoms persist, they can develop into PTSD, a long-term, often chronic, anxiety disorder.

Furthermore, in studies of populations who experienced a mass trauma such as that of the earthquake in Haiti, incidence rates of PTSD and other psychopathologies were significantly elevated over the rates of populations who had not experienced such an event. For example, studies of refugees have returned PTSD prevalence rates of more than 50%, in addition to other psychological disorders, and a study of several Beirut neighborhoods affected by widespread civil conflict found that over one-fifth of people who had experienced a fatal event (e.g., the loss of a loved one) developed PTSD and that PTSD was more likely to occur comorbidly with depression than to occur individually.

Although each situation and culture is unique, previous research indicates that responding policy makers and aid agencies working in southern Haiti should be prepared to encounter a society experiencing very high rates of PTSD and other psychopathologies. Since, as discussed previously, these disorders can have negative impacts on people's ability to participate in development and reconstruction initiatives, it is critical that health responders in particular work to first evaluate the incidence of trauma-related disorders and then to treat these problems in a culturally sensitive, efficient way.

Recovering from Trauma: Factors That Can Influence Outcomes

Scientific research with trauma survivors has revealed that there are factors that can either increase or decrease the likelihood that someone will develop a trauma-related mental illness following traumatic exposure. The severity and nearness of the trauma are strong indicators of whether or not a person will develop PTSD (e.g., did someone experience a car accident or an earthquake, did they witness something bad, or were they a victim themselves). In the case of interest to this brief, Haiti, hundreds of thousands of people have experienced firsthand an intense traumatic stressor, one that is compounded by the secondary traumas of continuing to live in unsafe conditions and, for many people, witnessing things like the death of a loved one. People who have experienced severe trauma, such as the one that has occurred in southern Haiti, are most likely to develop chronic disorders. Thus, the population in this area is at increased risk for long-term mental illness.

There are also pre-exposure factors that have been identified as potential mediators of pathological outcome. These include education level at time of exposure (increased education is a protective factor), family and personal mental health history, previous traumatic exposure (including experiences like family violence and prolonged food insecurity), and age at time of exposure (younger people are at higher risk for developing all manner of psychological difficulties immediately after trauma exposure and longitudinally, as well).

Haiti's pervasive poverty, recent history of violent political instability, and numerous natural disasters (including hurricanes and mudslides) prior to the earthquake all combine to create a populace that has likely been traumatized previously, making them more susceptible to trauma-related illness now. The fact that most Haitians are wholly uneducated deprives them of an additional protective factor. Port-au-Prince's enfants de rue, or street children, have seen their already significant numbers swell as more and more children are orphaned or abandoned in the wake of the quake (prior to the quake there were an estimated 50,000 children living on the streets of Port-au-Prince, and quite possibly more considering that UNICEF [the United Nations Children's Fund] reported 380,000 orphaned or abandoned children in Haiti before the quake). This group's young age, history of precarious living conditions, lack of education, and likely traumatic exposure prior to the earthquake will make them especially vulnerable to developing trauma-related illnesses.

Post-trauma factors can play a mediating role in pathological development. Level of perceived control over one's life (which is quite low at this moment for most people), the presence or absence of additional stressors (financial, physical health, interpersonal, etc., all of which are likely to be issues for the average earthquake victim), the speed with which a person is able to access health services after a traumatic event, and the presence and extent of social networks can all influence one's likelihood of developing a psychological disorder as a result of trauma. Among these factors, the most influential is often the social network; a larger, stronger social network can be a vital protective element. Although Haitians normally have a strong sense of community and especially of family obligation, these potential sources of assistance have been weakened by the deaths of family and friends and the relocation of others. It will be extremely important to assist victims in reinforcing what is left of their social networks or, in some cases, building entirely new ones. Additionally, increasing the number of medical staff and equipment on the ground can only help, particularly if mental health workers are available to augment the services provided by physical health workers. Ensuring that people receive prompt medical care could also assist in increasing their perceived level of control, which can decrease their likelihood of developing a trauma-related mental illness.

The fact that most Haitians are wholly uneducated deprives them of an additional protective factor.

In essence, Haiti at this moment lacks almost all protective factors, while there is an abundance of risk factors. This makes it far more likely that a significant percentage of the survivor population will experience a trauma-related mental illness in the future. It is therefore imperative that organizations responding to this crisis anticipate this need and work efficiently to establish culturally appropriate treatment and intervention services.

Mental Health in Haiti: Specific Issues

The issue of what is "culturally appropriate" can be somewhat nebulous, but it is an important consideration nonetheless. It is important to have an understanding of social norms and public perception of mental health issues while developing psychosocial programming. In the case of Haiti, there is a widespread stigma against mental illness; anyone professing to have an emotional disturbance is perceived as being "crazy."

Therefore, it will be necessary to not just start treatment services, but to prepare the population with some psychoeducation initiatives, using clinics and food distribution points to inform people about trauma and how it is not unusual to experience psychological distress afterward. Also, psychosocial, rather than strictly psychological, intervention methods may be more appropriate in this case for two reasons: First, because of the sheer number of people affected, it is not feasible

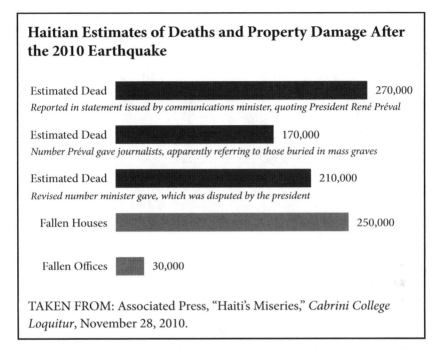

Haitian Estimates of Deaths and Property Damage After the 2010 Earthquake

Estimated Dead — 270,000
Reported in statement issued by communications minister, quoting President René Préval

Estimated Dead — 170,000
Number Préval gave journalists, apparently referring to those buried in mass graves

Estimated Dead — 210,000
Revised number minister gave, which was disputed by the president

Fallen Houses — 250,000

Fallen Offices — 30,000

TAKEN FROM: Associated Press, "Haiti's Miseries," *Cabrini College Loquitur*, November 28, 2010.

to attempt individual counseling for everyone. Second, more socially oriented therapeutic activities (e.g., group counseling, advocacy meetings, network building, or even sports) not only reach more people, but they can increase feelings of solidarity and empathy; they assist in promoting the very important social support network previously discussed; and they are less likely to be perceived as something clinical meant only for "crazy people."

Mental health practitioners working in this region should acquaint themselves ahead of time with Haitian social and spiritual practices (including vodou [a Haitian religion]) in order to have some understanding of how their clients may be thinking and feeling at this time. In particular, issues related to death, the afterlife, and what happens if someone is not buried "properly" are likely to be sources of extreme stress for many survivors, as well as potentially putting them at risk for experiencing complicated grief, a persistent, severe depressive state that often follows the untimely, unnatural, or unexpected death of a loved one. Also, most Haitians are devout Christians (either Catholic or Protestant) and frequently seek and find solace with religious leaders. It will be important for mental health practitioners to both set aside any prejudices they may have about religion and also for them to reach out to religious leaders, as they will be an ally in reaching people in need and encouraging them to seek help.

Mental health practitioners working in this region should acquaint themselves ahead of time with Haitian social and spiritual practices.

Post-Disaster Care

It is critical that even at this early stage of assistance, those involved in the effort are or become aware that the mental health needs will be massive, and that if these needs go unaddressed, rebuilding southern Haiti will be even more difficult than imagined, due to the negative social, economic, and physical health consequences of untreated mental illness. Many relevant lessons have been learned from academic research in the fields of clinical and community psychology, as well as the mental health response to past mass disasters including the September 11th terrorist attacks [in the United States in 2001], Hurricane Katrina [in New Orleans, Louisiana, in 2005], and the Asian tsunami of 2004. Previous research and experience have all demonstrated that it is important to plan and enact a mental health response to the Haiti earthquake in a prompt, organized manner.

Any assistance effort is of course dependent on the amount of human capacity and funding available, but in order to effectively manage the mental health consequences of this disaster, a well-ordered timeline of responsive programming will be needed. The following timeline is somewhat idealistic in that it envisions a tightly coordinated mental health response that is not always possible under such extreme conditions, as well as incorporating a policy-building aspect that may not be feasible in the near future. However, it is generally quite practical, drawing on suggestions made by professionals in community health, lessons learned from the use of psychological first aid after Hurricane Katrina, and focusing more on developing individual and group capacity and life skills instead of on traditional therapeutic methods that can be time and resource consuming and may not be culturally appropriate in this setting. To policy makers, funding agencies, and responding organizations, the following timeline—which is by no means rigid—is suggested:

0–3 months post-earthquake. Mental health should not be (and so far is not) a priority in and of itself. Focus should be on providing physical security (shelter, food, water, medical treatment), with only limited attention to emotional injuries. Physical medical personnel working in primary health care settings should be prepared to provide some psychological first aid to people presenting with symptoms such as nightmares, physical pain without physical cause, etc. This can include giving patients a brief orientation to relaxation techniques, identifying specific triggers that cause these symptoms, or helping people identify resources available to them, such as friends and family, food distribution points, etc. This will help decrease some of the negative symptomatology and enhance a person's perceived level of control, which has been shown to decrease the likelihood of a person developing chronic trauma-related illnesses.

The mental health needs will be massive.

3–6 months post-earthquake. Mental health specialists should begin providing specialized services, with plans developed for adults, children, and families. Mental states and prevalence rates could/should be evaluated using subjective

49

and standardized measures; this can be accomplished by surveying patients at medical clinics and/or through visits to the encampments throughout southern Haiti where most people are now living. If possible, these evaluations should be done in a coordinated, consistent manner, either through the formation of a mental health cluster (an organization of all agencies and actors providing mental health services) or by having one organization spearhead mental health initiatives. This will reduce duplication of services and, more importantly, help ensure that the population receives regular, reliable service instead of sporadic, unpredictable bursts.

Mental health specialists should also begin networking with religious leaders, community elders, and physical health care providers in the area. An explanation of services and psycho-education (specifically, raising public awareness and understanding of trauma and its effects) initiatives should be undertaken with the participation of these community leaders. This will assist in promoting the available services and making sure that people who may be in need are reached through one channel or another. Also, affiliation with such groups can help reduce the negative stigma attached to receiving mental health services; if someone's pastor or another respected figure assures them that they are not crazy if they seek help for their symptoms, they are more likely to do so.

Later Care

6–12 months post-earthquake. Mental health services should continue, adapting as they go along to the changing needs of the clients and the changing situation. If possible, people should be encouraged to seek work, to participate in rebuilding efforts, and/or to go to school; in essence, they should attempt to re-establish or start for the first time an active, regimented, productive schedule. This will help increase a sense of control and will provide a much-needed sense of normalcy. Building on the lessons delivered through psycho-education programs, community trainings could/should begin, wherein people are taught how to prepare for future disasters, including hurricanes, floods, and mudslides as well as earthquakes. Topics can include keeping a food and water store on hand, creating an activation network (similar to a phone tree, but involving in-person contact in the event that phones do not work) that groups can use to organize themselves, and identifying and/or building places that can provide shelter in the aftermath of future disasters. A smaller program could focus on training select community members in how to provide first aid—physical and psychological—to other people during and after emergencies. These trainings will serve the dual purpose of increasing social support and solidarity, while also giving people lifesaving skills to apply in the future. A coordinated effort to establish a modern, practical public mental health policy in Haiti could also be undertaken at this time. Although this work will continue for quite some time, it will be critical to seize the momentum created by this tragedy to ensure that Haiti is better prepared in the future to identify and properly treat its citizens who are experiencing mental illness, whether trauma related or not. In addition to skilled mental health professionals, this effort will need to include government officials, lawyers, and community leaders, among others.

12–18 months post-earthquake. Mental health services should continue as needed, but as clients begin to overcome their emotional wounds, programs focusing on empowerment, community organization, and appropriate methods of advocacy should begin. This will assist in facilitating a long-term societal recovery, not just individual. Public mental health policy initiatives should continue as well.

Beyond 18 months. All of these activities will likely need to continue indefinitely, as it will be quite some time before southern Haiti is able to rebuild, which means that the people residing in this area will be spending a protracted amount of time in extremely difficult living conditions, even by Haitian standards. Some Haitians may never develop a trauma-related illness and of those that do, a number will recover within the first year to eighteen months. However, the ongoing nature of this crisis is such that for many people, they may need psychological and psychosocial support for an extended period of time. Responding actors need to be prepared to maintain a long-term presence in this area, even in the face of frustration, resistance, and hardship.

Much of the population of southern Haiti will experience at least an acute trauma response, and the percentage of the population affected by long-term trauma-related mental illness will be significant. While care for physical needs is at this moment (three weeks after the event) of primary importance, it is necessary that responding actors begin planning even now for how to address the mental health fallout of this unprecedented disaster. Although it will take time to finalize the details of how to provide mental health assistance, on what scale to do so, and when certain activities should begin or end, what is indisputable is that at this very moment, awareness of these issues must be present and that at least some of the aid dollars being allotted now must be directed toward supporting a long-term mental health response. Otherwise, a Haitian society already scarred by decades of unrest, food insecurity, and deep poverty will find it enormously difficult to overcome their invisible wounds and participate in a meaningful, lasting way in the physical recovery of their much-beloved country. For though many of them will survive and will return to their old means of scraping together a living, they will be mired in the patterns of withdrawal, pessimism, and fear that characterize most trauma-related illnesses, leaving a population that is alive, but unable to envision a better future, let alone help build one.

Japan Needs to Respond Quickly and Effectively to Traumatic Stress Caused by Its Earthquake

Metin Basoglu

Metin Basoglu is head of trauma studies at the Institute of Psychiatry of King's College London and director of the Istanbul Centre for Behaviour Research and Therapy in Turkey. In the following viewpoint, he argues that natural disasters such as earthquakes can have serious, long-term psychological consequences. He also argues that earthquake trauma is the result of uncertainty and fear, not of blame or anger. He says that mental health interventions must confront the fear and teach people to cope with and overcome it. He asserts that these interventions are vital and must be based on research and knowledge of earthquake disasters specifically.

As you read, consider the following questions:

1. According to Basoglu, how long did traumatic stress persist in survivors of the 1999 Turkey earthquakes?

2. Why does Basoglu say that earthquake trauma is similar to trauma from torture?

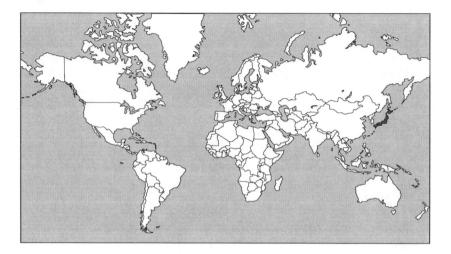

3. Why does Basoglu argue that psychological first aid is not likely to be effective for Japanese earthquake survivors?

In [a previous blog post] I had pointed to ill-informed comments from mental health professionals about the mental health effects of the Japan disaster [referring to the March 2011 earthquake and tsunami]. I will expand on this issue a bit further by highlighting how "expert" opinion on this issue is plagued by various common misconceptions about earthquake trauma. There are numerous examples of this in the media but I will focus on only a select few.

Man-Made vs. Natural Disasters

A *New York Times* [NYT] article—"Lessons for Japan's Survivors: The Psychology of Recovery"—based on expert opinions illustrates some of the most common misconceptions in the field of psychological trauma. There are several unsubstantiated assumptions in expert statements. First, that man-made disasters have more lasting psychological effects than natural disasters is not based on any evidence. There are no studies comparing long-term effects of different types of disaster.

Second, the view that man-made trauma has more cognitive effects than natural disasters—such as blame, guilt, loss of faith in people, etc.—is not supported by evidence. Our studies show that earthquake survivors do not differ from torture survivors in this respect. In fact, over 90% of earthquake survivors we have assessed in our studies blamed local or national government authorities for allowing construction of substandard buildings, as well as for delayed or inadequate rescue and relief efforts. Their feelings of anger, resentment, demoralization, disillusionment, distrust, loss of faith in people, and pessimism were similar to those we observed in torture survivors both in frequency and intensity.

Third, the article states: "After purely natural disasters, about 95 percent of those directly affected typically shake off disabling feelings of sadness or grief in the first year, experts say; just eight months after Hurricane Ivan leveled Orange Beach, Ala., in 2004, about three-quarters of people thought the town was back on track, researchers found."

Although such comments may inspire hope, unfortunately, many studies show that this is not the case with earthquake survivors. Our studies with more than 4,000 survivors of the 1999 earthquakes in Turkey show that traumatic stress problems in the community persist for at least 40 months after the disaster. Indeed, over 50% of the survivors we contacted three years after the disaster needed help and requested treatment from us.

The view that man-made trauma has more cognitive effects than natural disasters . . . is not supported by evidence.

Interventions Are Necessary

The view that most survivors will recover spontaneously implies that no interventions are necessary for most people in the early stages of the disaster. This is also not true for earthquake survivors. Earthquake survivors are desperate for help in the early stages of the disaster mainly because of pervasive and debilitating fear. Indeed, when we set up a treatment delivery project in the epicenter region, we were inundated by requests for help from so many survivors that we were compelled to develop very brief and largely self-help-based interventions for them. We treated with good results many survivors in the acute phase of the disaster—namely within the first year during which they experienced a second major earthquake and hundreds of aftershocks. This helped them gain resilience against the effects of ongoing trauma. Such early and effective intervention is critical in preventing chronic traumatic stress, depression, and other health problems.

Earthquake survivors are desperate for help in the early stages of the disaster mainly because of pervasive and debilitating fear.

With its focus on cognitive effects of trauma, such as blame, anger, frustration, sense of injustice, the NYT article gives the impression that the psychological effects of the Japan disaster is likely to last decades. While it is true that such cognitive effects and related emotions may last a very long time, what is overlooked is the fact that such trauma effects are secondary to traumatic stress, i.e., fear, distress, and helplessness. In other words, people do not have traumatic stress because of such cognitive effects. Rather, they develop these beliefs and associated emotions because of traumatic stress. This implies that, with effective treatment of the causal process, their thinking is likely to change. There is indeed evidence to support this point. The NYT article totally misses this important point and portrays an unduly pessimistic picture about the long-term outcome of the disaster. Having said this, I should also add that this prediction could turn out to be true (for different reasons though), if the survivors do not receive appropriate treatment for traumatic stress.

It is also important to note that the problem of radiation leak in Japan[1] is likely to make the psychological impact of the disaster worse through augmenting people's fear and not because "many people ... have begun to doubt the official versions of events" or that "... people are getting angrier because of the inaccurate information they're getting." If the radiation leak incident had not occurred, such distrust of authorities and anger would have been as common among Japanese survivors for other reasons. This is because people have a natural tendency to attribute blame to other people even when the disaster is not of human design.

Pointing to the risks of "one-on-one therapy and crisis counseling efforts" the article quotes a medical anthropologist and psychiatric epidemiologist at the University of California, Davis: "We have to be careful that we don't create a whole class of victims, that we don't put people into some diagnostic box that makes them permanently dependent."

This statement is no more than a cliché shared by many in the field of psychological trauma. Although it may come across as a "politically correct" view, it serves to de-emphasize the importance of individual psychological interventions in helping people recover from trauma. As I noted in my first post, such interventions are of paramount importance in facilitating recovery from trauma, provided that the right treatment is chosen. Traumatic stress is not a *diagnostic box*; it is a real problem that affects millions of people after major disasters. What makes survivors *permanently dependent* is depriving them of effective interventions.

Earthquake Trauma Is Distinct

This brief analysis of a few but a rather representative sample of comments highlights the state of current knowledge in the

---

1. The earthquake damaged Japanese nuclear reactors, resulting in serious radiation leaks.

The 2011 Japanese Tsunami

Within an hour after the approximately five-minute earth-quake finally stopped, officials issued a tsunami warning. The warning went out not only to Japan, but to 50 other countries including the West Coast of the United States. A tsunami is a series of huge waves that are created offshore by the movement of undersea earthquakes or volcanoes, and then move toward land. The waves move outward in concentric rings and can affect any area whose coast touches the body of water where the tsunami began. The waves often reach incredible heights as they crash onto the shore and drag everything in their path back toward the sea. Japan's earthquake spawned a tsunami with waves more than 30 feet (9 m) high. Some of the waves washed inland six miles (10 km) from the coast. Within just a few minutes of the wave's appearance, the damage was widespread. Cars, boats, and trains were swept away. Bridges and roads collapsed. Houses were destroyed.

Marcia Amidon Lüsted, The 2011 Japan Disasters,
Edina, MN: ABDO Publishing Company, 2012, pp. 8–10.

field. Furthermore, most Western trauma researchers do not have sufficient experience with major devastating earthquakes. Those with such experience often do not have recourse to a sound theory in understanding how earthquake trauma impacts people. Those with experience with other disasters often believe that such experience is easily transferrable to work with earthquake survivors. This is not the case. Earthquake trauma has important features that distinguish it from other disasters. Our comparative studies show that the immediate and long-term psychological effects of earthquakes are almost indistinguishable from those of torture trauma. This is because both trauma events share the same characteristic: a strong element of unpredictability and uncontrollability. Consequently, both lead to widespread and severe helplessness responses. This is not true for most other disasters.

Earthquake-induced traumatic stress runs a chronic course in a substantial proportion of survivors. This is to be expected, considering that aftershocks continue for a long time—at times more than a year. Furthermore, fear of future earthquakes does not easily subside in a seismically active region. Further earthquakes in the region often sustain and reinforce the traumatic effects of the previous disaster. . . .

The focus of attention in any mental health care approach to earthquake trauma needs to be on fear and related traumatic stress problems. To highlight this issue, I will use a news story by Reuters. Here is an excerpt:

> "Many people cannot sleep well at night as they are afraid of earthquakes. They have lost many things so they are psychologically hurt," doctor Keiichiro Kubota told Reuters at a makeshift clinic in Kesennuma.
>
> The difficulty of comforting survivors is compounded by the more than 350 aftershocks recorded since March 11.
>
> "I am sleeping with my regular clothes on. I am always feeling an earthquake. Even when a car passes by, I think it's an earthquake," said Toshie Fukuda, 64, a survivor in Rikuzentakata, one of the cities hit hardest by the tsunami.
>
> At the main disaster evacuee center in Rikuzentakata, a junior high school, the psychological counseling center is a curtained-off 4 square meter (36 sq ft) corner of a classroom.
>
> "Do you suffer from headaches, stomach aches, diarrhea? Are you easily agitated and unable to sleep? Do you have no appetite, suffer nightmares about the disaster, or lack your normal energy? Are you irritated by the smallest sound, unable to stop crying and unable to relax?" reads a clinic poster.

"These feelings are not at all unusual—they are the normal reaction of people who have received a severe shock," the poster said. "Talk to a specialist to lighten your burden."

The problems described here represent a symptom profile that is very characteristic of earthquake trauma. Pervasive fear caused by expectations of another earthquake—reinforced by ongoing aftershocks—leads to sleeping problems, avoidance behaviors (e.g., sleeping with clothes on), and extreme alertness and startle responses (e.g., in response to vibrations caused by cars passing by). Although these symptoms are accompanied by some other PTSD [post-traumatic stress disorder] symptoms (not mentioned in the Reuters article), these problems are at the core of earthquake-related PTSD. Other symptoms mentioned in the story stem from intense fear.

Pervasive fear caused by expectations of another earthquake ... leads to sleeping problems, avoidance behaviors (e.g., sleeping with clothes on), and extreme alertness and startle responses.

Survivors often avoid a wide range of situations where they are either reminded of the trauma experiences during the earthquake or where they think they might get caught up in another earthquake. We found that they avoid on average about 15 different situations (including even sexual intercourse) because of associated fear or distress. Such extensive avoidance aggravates feelings of helplessness; causes significant functional impairment in work, social, and family life; and very quickly leads to depression. Research shows that all this can be effectively prevented in over 90% of survivors by helping them overcome their fear or distress by *not avoiding feared situations and distressing trauma reminders*. It is as simple as that! Such intervention increases sense of control over trauma, reduces helplessness, and leads to generalized improvement in all life domains affected by the trauma.

Misunderstanding Persists

We have reported all these research findings in more than 20 publications in the last 10 years. Yet, unfortunately, such knowledge does not seem to have sunk in. It is worth mentioning in this connection an article posted on the American Psychological Association website noting that psychological first aid is a vital intervention for Japanese survivors. To my knowledge, there is no evidence to show that this intervention is useful in earthquake survivors. It is not likely to be useful, because it lacks a therapy element specifically designed to tackle the causal process in earthquake-induced traumatic stress: fear. . . . You need antibiotics to treat an infection; aspirin will not work!

Earthquake-induced fears are often of phobic quality, irrational, beyond cognitive control, and therefore resistant to any intervention lacking such a critical element. Informing survivors about how they can avoid helplessness by confronting such fears needs to be the first intervention in the early aftermath of an earthquake before fear becomes pervasive and extensive avoidance sets in.

A *USA Today* article says that the Japanese Red Cross has 2,400 nurses trained to provide psychosocial support after disasters. It also says

> One tool mental health workers in Japan could use is the U.S. Department of Veterans Affairs' and the National Child Traumatic Stress Network's Psychological First Aid: Field Operations Guide, which has been translated into Japanese and is available online. It is designed to reduce stress and help people function better immediately after a disaster and includes 17 pages of handouts covering such topics as the value of social support to relaxation tips and advice on easing kids' fears.

Unfortunately, none of this is likely to help survivors, given that psychosocial support alone or relaxation is not conducive to substantial recovery from traumatic stress.

The same article refers to the American Psychological Association, which apparently advised the following: "the U.S. psychologists with disaster response experience should stay home unless they've been formally invited to help survivors of the March 11 quake and tsunami and are proficient in Japan's language and culture."

This is sound advice! I would however propose a minor amendment to make it even more sound: *Stay home unless you have something useful to offer!*

To conclude, Japan needs to undertake a mental health care program without further delay and start planning for long-term care services for survivors. Mental health professionals need to consider the fact that their experiences with trauma survivors may not necessarily apply to earthquake trauma and exercise more caution in their comments to the media. Ill-informed comments are likely to mislead care providers, governments, and other organizations concerned with survivor care, leading them to underestimate the gravity of the problem. Similarly, the media needs to adopt more responsible reporting by seeking comments from appropriately qualified mental health professionals.

The Lingering Effects of Torture: Scientists Assess the Long-Term Effects of Torture on the Human Mind

Devin Powell

Devin Powell is a writer whose work has appeared on Antiwar .com and in Science News. *In the following viewpoint, he says that recent research has shown that psychological torture can be as damaging in its long-term effects as physical torture. Powell says it has been very difficult to study the effects of torture but that researchers have begun to make some progress. Research suggests that the main cause of trauma is not physical violence but rather a loss of control. Powell asserts that therapy has been shown to help victims of torture recover from trauma.*

As you read, consider the following questions:

1. To what torture was Adeel subjected in US custody, according to Powell?

2. Why does Powell say that it is very difficult to link a specific form of torture directly to long-term psychological problems?

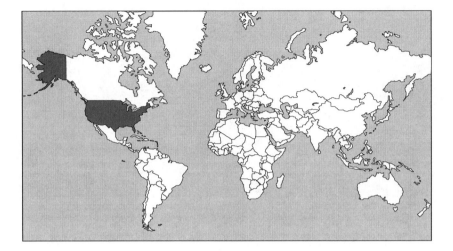

3. According to the viewpoint, torture survivors are comparable to groups who survive what kinds of disasters?

Like many of the other inmates interrogated at Guantánamo Bay, Adeel's personal nightmare did not end when he returned home.

Today, in his native Pakistan, the sound of approaching footsteps or the sight of someone in a uniform can trigger bad memories and set off a panic attack. The former teacher and father of five now thinks of himself as a suspicious and lonely person.

"I feel like I am in a big prison and still in isolation. I have lost all my life," he told psychologists working for the nonprofit Physicians for Human Rights. They diagnosed him as having post-traumatic stress disorder (PTSD) and severe depression.

Newly emerging research on large numbers of torture survivors shows that anecdotal stories like these are common and suggests that "psychological" forms of torture—often thought to be milder than the direct infliction of physical pain—can in fact have serious long-term mental health consequences.

Adeel's story is similar to those of other prisoners who may be released this year as President Obama pushes to close the facility. Adeel spent four years in U.S. custody, first at the Bagram Theater Internment Facility in Afghanistan and then at Guantánamo—and was freed in 2006, never having been charged with a crime.

"I feel like I am in a big prison and still in isolation. I have lost all my life."

Adeel said that while in U.S. custody he was sexually humiliated and wrapped in a hood, goggles, earphones, and gloves that cut off his senses during a 24-hour flight. His descriptions of what happened match many of the practices that U.S. officials said were used at the prisons. Adeel said he was kept in isolation in a chilled cell, blasted with loud music to prevent him from sleeping, and forced to stand motionless in the hot sun for hours.

"For two months I couldn't sleep because there was a very strong light. . . . If you fell asleep just for a few minutes they played very loud American music, so you could not sleep," the man who now goes by the alias Adeel recalled in a recent report by the Physicians for Human Rights.

Memos sent in 2002 from the U.S. Department of Justice to the CIA, released earlier this year by President Obama, describe these and other interrogation techniques—such as tossing prisoners against flexible walls and using waterboarding. These techniques, which leave few physical marks, are also used to toughen American troops undergoing survival, evasion, resistance, and escape training. After consulting with the military officers who run these programs, the CIA concluded that "none of these [officers] was aware of any prolonged psychological effect caused by the use of any of the . . . techniques either separately or as a course of conduct," according to one of the memos.

The Tortured Mind

Psychologists and neuroscientists, on the other hand, tend to argue that techniques do cause long-term harm. But what can science actually show about the effects of "psychological" torture on civilians like Adeel years after their real-world interrogations?

Linking a specific form of torture directly to long-term psychological problems is very difficult to do because of the ethics of experimenting on humans. Because scientists cannot torture subjects in the laboratory and check for long-term effects, they study real-world survivors of torture, such as refugees from war-torn countries and former prisoners of war, each of whom has experienced a variety of traumatic experiences.

Previous work suggested that the distinction between the harshness of "physical" torture and the mildness of "psychological" torture is a false one.

Doctors who work with these victims often rely not on scientific studies but on their own personal observations to assess the long-term impacts of a particular experience. Harvard psychiatrist Stuart Grassian, who studies prisoners put into solitary confinement, believes from his own personal experience that "people [put into solitary confinement] become loners." Years after being removed from solitary confinement, "they tend to become irritable, hypervigilant, jumpy, fearful and chronically tense." But when asked to testify in a class-action suit against "supermax" prisons that use solitary confinement, he found few scientific studies to support these beliefs. Research that tried to isolate the impact of solitary confinement on American soldiers kept in Korean P.O.W. camps, for example, was largely inconclusive. Its analysis was complicated by the fact that people put in solitary confinement are usually mistreated in other ways as well.

New research that tries to untangle the horrors suffered by torture survivors was recently presented at the 11th European Conference on Traumatic Stress in Oslo, Norway. Metin Basoglu, a psychiatrist at King's College London, described the statistical techniques he used to single out the mental impacts of "cruel, inhuman, and degrading treatments" that range from threats and isolation to electric shocks and beatings on the feet.

His previous work suggested that the distinction between the harshness of "physical" torture and the mildness of "psychological" torture is a false one. When torture victims from the former Yugoslavia rated the distress caused by different forms of abuse on a scale from zero to four, those techniques that did not involve physical pain were just as distressing, or even slightly more so, than those that directly inflicted pain. "The threat or anticipation of pain may be worse than the pain itself," said Basoglu.

Painful Combination

Basoglu's latest and largest study looked for links between a person's perception of the severity of an experience and the likelihood of later developing PTSD, the most common disorder associated with torture.

Combinations that predicted PTSD included putting people in stressful, helpless positions to maximize the impacts of verbal threats and stripping their clothes off to enhance the humiliation of being sprayed with cold water.

By studying hundreds of political dissidents from Turkey and military prisoners of war of the former Yugoslavia—all of whom were tortured—Basoglu discovered that deceptively banal mistreatments that may not cause long-term psychological problems when used individually can lead to mental disorders when grouped together or inflicted sequentially.

Consider a situation in which a prisoner is slapped across the face while wearing a hood with his hands tied behind his back. Alone, none of these abuses—slapping, hooding, or hand-tying—can predict whether that person will develop a long-term mental disorder. But when the techniques are grouped together, said Basoglu, their effects multiply and raise the likelihood of developing PTSD. The psychological trauma of being slapped in the face is made much worse by a blindfold and handcuffs, which prevent victims from anticipating and shielding themselves against the blow.

"We find strong correlations between clusters of events and mental health outcomes," said Basoglu.

Other combinations that predicted PTSD included putting people in stressful, helpless positions to maximize the impacts of verbal threats and stripping their clothes off to enhance the humiliation of being sprayed with cold water.

Psychologist Claudia Catani looked for traces of these long-term clinical problems in the brains of torture survivors at the rehabilitation centers of the University of Konstanz in Germany.

Using a technique that detects magnetic fields created by electrical activity in the brain, Catani compared the patterns of brain activity of non-traumatized people to those of people who had experienced torture and who had subsequently developed PTSD. She found distinct differences in the area of the brain that controls attention that suggest torture victims are more sensitive to the sight of a potential threat.

Some psychologists have argued that, when shown a picture of something horrific like a massacre or a violent act, someone with PTSD will have a stronger reaction because the part of the brain that controls attention will become overactive and fixate on the image.

But Catani found the exact opposite to be the case. The brain activity in torture victims responding to the photos shows that they actually pay less attention to a threatening photo, not that they fixate. Her explanation is that PTSD sufferers carry traumatic experiences deep in their emotional memory and consciousnesses, programming them to react more quickly and strongly to threatening scenes.

"[P]ictures with such explicit contents as war and attack scenes are immediately categorized as a threat and do not require sustained visual processing," said Catani.

Taking Control

Basoglu and Catani both agree that the underlying principle that makes torture so traumatic is the individual's loss of control. Comparing torture to other kinds of trauma, torture survivors tend to be just as likely to develop mental disorders as people who have survived similarly uncontrollable events like massive earthquakes or plane crashes. "Our data on this is unpublished, but it is the first time someone has compared these groups," said Basoglu.

"If you don't do anything about the clinical condition, these long-term effects do not go away," said Catani. But the good news for people trying to rebuild their lives is that various forms of psychotherapy have been shown in clinical trials to help.

Periodical and Internet Sources Bibliography

The following articles have been selected to supplement the diverse views presented in this chapter.

Associated Press
"Japan's Quake Survivors Need Mental Care: Report," CBC News, June 10, 2011.

Associated Press
"Most Holocaust Survivors Battle Depression," MSNBC.com, January 26, 2010.

Katherine Harmon
"Are Infectious Diseases Now Really Haiti's Biggest Health Threat?," *Scientific American*, January 15, 2010.

Molly Hennessy-Fiske
"Tackling Mental Health Problems in Afghanistan," *Los Angeles Times*, May 15, 2011.

Courtney Hutchison
"Healing Japan: Psychological Fallout Could Last Years," ABC News, March 17, 2011.

Suzanne Kianpour and David Willis
"Afghan Rampage Prompts PTSD Debate in US Military Town," BBC News, March 19, 2012.

Cordula Meyer
"What Joe Dwyer's Death Can Teach Us About PTSD," *Spiegel Online*, March 25, 2010. www.spiegel.de.

Richard F. Mollica
"Surviving Torture," *New England Journal of Medicine*, vol. 351, July 1, 2004.

Mark Phillips
"Britain Limits Deployment to Reduce P.T.S.D.," *New York Times*, March 20, 2012.

Julia Robinson Shimizu
"The Trauma of Mental Illness," *Los Angeles Times*, August 24, 2009.

Deborah Sontag
"In Haiti, Mental Health System Is in Collapse," *New York Times*, March 19, 2010.

Mental Illness and Human Rights

In Israel, as Worldwide, the Mentally Ill Face Stigma and Discrimination

Amir Tal, David Roe, and Patrick W. Corrigan

Amir Tal is a researcher in the Israel Ministry of Industry, Trade, and Labor and a cofounder and editor of Stigma Research and Action; *David Roe is the chair of the Department of Community Mental Health at the University of Haifa; and Patrick W. Corrigan is a professor of psychology at the Illinois Institute of Technology. In the following viewpoint, they argue that stigma against people with mental illness is prevalent worldwide and that it is also a major problem in Israel. They say that the stigma against the mentally ill is expressed by everyone from landlords to police to mental health professionals. This stigma, the authors claim, makes it harder to rehabilitate the mentally ill and that steps must be taken to combat it.*

As you read, consider the following questions:

1. What evidence do the authors present for the existence of stigma against the mentally ill in America and Germany?

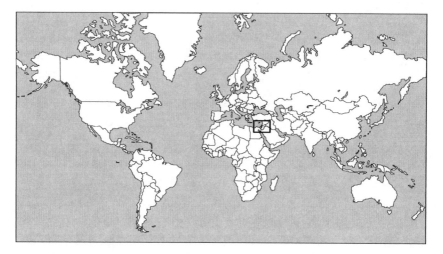

2. What do Israelis see as the most common characteristics of persons with mental illness, according to the authors?

3. What stigma do the authors say is faced by families of the mentally ill in Israel?

'Owth' (Genesis 4:15) means a sign, omen, warning or remembrance, and refers to the biblical passage where God declared that Cain was cursed. The modern use of 'mark of Cain' labels persons with a distinguishing characteristic and, in the process, devalues them. Throughout history, the label of mental illness has similarly marked persons and differentiated them from those without a mental illness. This 'mark', or stigma, refers to negative stereotyped beliefs, prejudice and behaviors toward persons with mental illness. Stereotyping and prejudice, in turn, may result in barriers to consumers' access to knowledgeable health care, treatment, social resources, social inclusion and opportunities for recovery. Negative attitudes and behavior toward persons with mental illness, which are often internalized by consumers, frequently generate feelings of shame, guilt, low self-esteem, social dependence, isolation and hopelessness. Moreover, underutilization of mental health services is one of the main consequences of stigma. Social behaviors that stigmatize persons with mental illness may impede their willingness to use those services that they could otherwise benefit from.

Psychiatric rehabilitation in Israel, similar to that in other countries, emphasizes support services and skills training to facilitate consumers' opportunity to set and pursue personal goals, including attempts to fulfill work, family, social and community roles. The rehabilitation services offered, however, focus almost exclusively on the person trying to recover, paying little attention to the context in which recovery occurs. [P.E.] Deegan has stressed the importance of not only directing efforts toward the individual's rehabilitation, but also enlarging the mainstream to accommodate persons with diverse functional capabilities, and leaves 'no one stranded on the fringes'. Hence, strategies for recovery and community integration of persons with mental illness must expand beyond rehabilitation services to include efforts to increase social inclusion and access for persons with mental illness while decreasing stereotyping, prejudice and discrimination. . . .

A Brief Overview of the Current Worldwide Situation

Stereotypes, prejudice and discrimination against persons with mental illness are common phenomena in Western culture. For example, 75% of the American public view persons with mental illness as dangerous. In a study conducted in Germany, almost two-thirds of respondents shared the view that 'former mental patients' are disadvantaged when it comes to applying for a job or dating and over half believed that persons in German society think less of a person who has been hospitalized in a 'mental hospital'. In a Canadian survey of attitudes toward disabilities, respondents reported that, of all disabilities, they were much less comfortable when in the presence of someone with a mental illness. For example, the greatest degree of comfort is associated with 'physical' disabilities (i.e.,

80% would feel very or somewhat comfortable around someone using a wheelchair) while it is less comfortable being around persons with 'hidden' or 'internal' disabilities (i.e., 46% would feel very or somewhat comfortable around someone with chronic depression). Two-thirds of the public surveyed in Switzerland favored revoking drivers' licenses of persons with mental illness. In a survey of consumers in the United Kingdom, 70% reported that either they or a family member had experienced stigma as a result of mental illness. Of those, 56% experienced stigma within their own family, 52% from friends, 44% from their primary care physician, 32% from other health care professionals and 30% in their workplace. Recent studies indicate that mental health professionals hold negative stereotypes (i.e., persons with mental illness are more 'dangerous', 'unpredictable', 'unreliable', 'lazy' than the general public), stigmatizing attitudes (i.e., low expectations about long outcomes and prognosis), and display a high level of social distance (i.e., unwillingness to interact with/live next to/marry/have children with a person with mental illness) toward persons with mental illness. In some studies, mental health professionals displayed the same or higher levels of negative stereotypes and social distance toward persons with mental illness than the general public.

As a result of the growing awareness of how common and universal stigma is, along with a growing appreciation of its devastating consequences, advocacy groups and anti-stigma programmes around the world have increased. Well-known campaigns are those in Australia, the United Kingdom, the United States, Canada, New Zealand, and the Global Program Against Stigma and Discrimination Because of Schizophrenia, launched by the World Psychiatric Association (WPA).

As evident from this brief review, stigma is, unfortunately, a common and widespread phenomenon. There is, however, an increasing awareness and appreciation of its devastating consequences, and a growing effort to combat it. Next we will discuss the current situation in the mental health field in Israel.

The Current Status of Programmes in Israel

In Israel, the public's awareness of mental health issues, and the stigma attached to it, has increased in recent years. This increase happened mostly due to mental health reforms, such as shifting the locus of care from psychiatric hospitals to care in community-based facilities and the growing number of mental health rehabilitation services in the community. More Israelis with mental illnesses are living in the community and can make use of rehabilitation services for supportive education, supported employment and housing in the community.

This positive shift toward growing community services strengthened the community's influence on the rehabilitation process, and the recovery and social inclusion of persons with mental illness. However, Israeli mental health services focus almost exclusively on one side of the equation, namely on interventions for consumers. There is an unmet need in Israel to integrate lessons learned from anti-stigma programmes in other locations into the rehabilitation process to overcome community barriers and to increase the access to services, opportunities for integration and active citizenship for persons with mental illness.

The results of this oversight are evident in the findings from recent Israeli studies on the public's attitude and behaviors toward persons with mental illness. Studies indicate that the Israeli public holds negative, stereotyping attitudes and that there is evidence of discriminatory behaviors toward persons with mental illness.

[N.] Struch et al. surveyed a sample of Israeli adults aged 21 and older to examine their attitudes toward persons with mental illness. When participants were asked which are the most common characteristics of persons with mental illness, more than 50% replied that persons with mental illness demonstrate 'bizarre behavior, language irregularities and unkempt personal appearance'. Eighty per cent mentioned that persons with mental illness are 'unpredictable'. Moreover, while 64% agreed that persons with mental illness can work, 58% thought that they *cannot* work in a normal job, such as a bank clerk. Behavior patterns revealed the well-documented NIMBY (Not in My Back Yard) phenomenon: 40% replied that they would not want a person with mental illness living in their neighborhood; 88% said that they would not let a person with mental illness take their children to school; and 50% replied that they are willing to help a person with mental illness but are not willing to be his or her friend.

There is an unmet need in Israel to integrate lessons learned from anti-stigma programmes in other locations into the rehabilitation process to overcome community barriers.

These findings indicate that the public holds negative attitudes and behavior toward persons with mental illness, which are likely to act as a major barrier in their rehabilitation process, recovery and social inclusion.

In the following section, we review the major barriers to rehabilitation and social inclusion of persons with mental illness identified in the professional literature—while emphasizing their relevance to Israeli efforts to promote access and life opportunities of persons with mental illness.

Barriers to Rehabilitation

Israeli society is similar to that of other countries and cultures where the general public stereotypes and stigmatizes persons with mental illness, and, as a result, may block opportunities for them to assume community roles. The professional literature shows that specific groups emerge as potential barriers to promotion of mental health interventions. These groups, usually referred to as power groups, are defined as groups whose attitudes about, and behaviors toward, persons with mental illness have a significant impact on their life opportunities. Hence, the most effective anti-stigma programmes are tailored to the specific perceptions, concerns, behaviors and contexts of the power group. Those groups are: landlords, employers, criminal justice professionals, persons with mental illness who adopt self-stigmatization, families of persons with mental illness, health care providers, public policy makers and the media.

First we want to refer to the Hebrew terminology for mental illness due to its potential effect on the attitude and behavior of power groups toward persons with mental illness. The Hebrew term for mental illness ('machalat nefesh') means the 'disease of the soul'. As stressed by [I.] Levav et al., this term is highly dissonant with current scientific concepts whereby mental disorders are recognized as biopsychosocial entities. Using the word soul ('nefesh') may suggest that the spiritual essence of a person is affected by the psychiatric disorder and that the dreams, hopes, love and decisions of persons with mental illness are diseased. The 'soul approach' may also add to the metaphysical characteristic of mental illness, an approach that is common among religious persons, both Jews and Muslim Arabs.

Landlords. Safe, reliable shelter is a basic human need. Unfortunately, many persons with mental illness are unable to obtain housing. Landlords may refuse to rent to persons with mental illness, or may block independent housing goals by not permitting reasonable accommodations. In other cases, persons from the community, and policy makers, are blocking housing options of persons with mental illness.

In recent years, the Israeli press has reported incidents where community members protested against hostels and other community-based housing for persons with mental illness. In at least one case, the protests escalated into burning and destruction of an existing hostel for persons with mental illness and retardation. Local residents have appealed to mayors and other politicians to prevent hostels in their neighborhoods. As a result of residents' pressure, some mayors promote legislation that will limit community-based housing for persons with mental illness or with substance abuse disorders.

Employers. Holding a job provides an important opportunity to function in society as an adult and contributes to building a social network. Moreover, a salary helps to improve quality of life and to prevent living in poverty, a common consequence of mental illness. Unfortunately, many employers hold negative attitudes toward persons with mental illness, and as a result are unwilling to hire or provide reasonable accommodations. One of the most critical barriers to the employment of persons with mental illness is the degree of social stigma and thus is connected to most employment-related problems: even though the majority of persons with mental disorders desire regular work, their unemployment rates are three to five times higher than among those without mental disorders; consumers are concerned about losing Supplemental Security Income (SSI) and Social Security Disability Insurance (SSDI) benefits; they feel embarrassed about symptoms and side effects of medications; they lack the training and skills necessary for certain jobs; and they have inculcated low expectations communicated to them from support staff and others.

According to the Commission for Equal Rights of Persons with Disabilities (State of Israel, Ministry of Justice, 2006), employment rates of persons with disabilities are very low when compared with the rest of the population. Persons with disabilities work more often than others in part-time positions, lower-paying occupations, and receive less professional training. Moreover, income from employment and job security are very low compared with those without disabilities. Lastly, in old age, the employment rates of persons with disabilities are negligible compared with the 20% that are employed from the rest of the population at the same ages. The National Insurance Institute report for 2005 indicates that the largest group of persons who receive general disability allowances are persons with psychiatric disabilities (31% of total recipients). In this large group of 50,000 persons with psychiatric disabilities, 2,559 work in sheltered workshops; 2,242 work in prevocational training; 1,286 work in supportive employment and 37 persons work in intensive sheltered workshops. These figures show that most of the mental health consumers in Israel work in 'shelter workshops', which involves monotonous and simple tasks, and provides little income.

More Power Groups

Criminal justice professionals. One of the most common stereotypes of persons with mental illness is that they are likely to be violent and dangerous. This stereotype may cause police officers to be overly defensive and may lead to overreactions toward persons with mental illness. Moreover, officers have the power to decide whether persons with mental illness receive adequate psychiatric care, remain in their current situation or are further processed into the criminal justice system. Therefore, police need specialized training to be able to recognize the signs of mental illness and to take appropriate actions.

Lastly, when persons with mental illness are victims, they often do not report the crime. When they do report a crime, they are often viewed as unreliable witnesses and little is done to assist them.

According to the Israeli public defender, in recent years, police refer persons with mental illness to the criminal justice system instead of to psychiatric care. Moreover, there is an increase of court orders for admissions to compulsory ambula-

Strategies to Reduce Stigma Against the Mentally Ill

Anti-stigma Strategies	Objectives
Education	Challenge inaccurate stereotypes about mental illness and replace them with factual information.
Contact	Facilitate interpersonal contact between persons with mental illness and members of the target group.
Protest	Frame the moral injustice of continued prejudice and discrimination; then instruct members of the target group to suppress the attitude.
Consequences	Reward people for positive expectations and affirmative actions. Withhold rewards for stigmatizing attitudes and discriminatory behavior.

These strategies were adopted from Patrick W. Corrigan's *Beat the Stigma and Discrimination! Four Lessons for Mental Health Advocates.*

Amir Tal, David Roe, and Patrick W. Corrigan, "Mental Illness Stigma in the Israeli Context: Deliberations and Suggestions," International Journal of Social Psychiatry, 2007, p. 8.

tory treatment (i.e., from 29 in 1996 to 108 in 2005), court observation orders (i.e., from 748 in 1999 to 968 in 2005) and court hospitalization order (i.e., from 165 in 1999 to 295 in 2005). Often, the cases that are transferred to the criminal justice system are 'easy' cases such as phone harassments and threats.

Policy makers. Policy makers in private and government institutions may restrict opportunities for persons with mental illness. The end results are to limit options of persons with mental illness and prevent their integration into society.

As in most countries, including the United States, mental health in Israel is underfunded; there is an inherent discrimination in private and public health insurance; one-third of persons who are entitled by law to public mental health services do not get them; and evidence-based interventions (that is, specific treatments with demonstrated efficacy) are not incorporated into clinical practice or into community-based programmes.

One of the most common stereotypes of persons with mental illness is that they are likely to be violent and dangerous.

Health care providers. Stigmatization of and discrimination against persons with mental illness are common among health care providers, including psychiatrists, social workers and psychologists. A recent study comparing knowledge of and attitudes toward persons with schizophrenia and major depression among mental health professionals and the general public found that psychiatrists had significantly more negative stereotypes than all other groups (i.e., psychologists, nurses, other therapists and the general public). Moreover, professionals displayed an equally high level of social distance toward persons with schizophrenia as the general public. Bias against persons with mental illness and their families can start early in professional training programmes and may lead to stigma, low expectations, infantilization and dehumanizing clinical practices, all damaging the work of recovery, healing and rebuilding consumers' lives. First-person accounts of Israeli consumers describe their experiences with stigmatizing attitudes and behaviors from mental health providers. These stories describe abuses (i.e., physical and emotional) in the mental health system, dehumanization behaviors from the professional staff and a strong feeling of paternalism and lack of respect.

The media. In all media worldwide, persons with mental illness are represented as violent, dangerous, unpredictable and criminal like. [H.] Stuart demonstrated that negative media images impair consumers' self-esteem, help-seeking behaviors, medication adherence and overall recovery. In contrast, the media have the potential to challenge public prejudices, initiate public debate and project positive, human-interest stories about persons who live with mental illness. To date [2007] no research has been conducted in Israel about this subject.

The Mentally Ill and Their Families

Many persons with mental illness accept negative stereotypes and prejudices, and apply those to themselves in a process of self-stigmatization. Self-stigmatization has a profound impact on the person with mental illness and may lead to low self-esteem, hopelessness, low self-confidence, unwillingness to seek help, treatment discontinuation, avolition [lack of motivation], shame and social isolation. These negative consequences of self-stigma worsen the course of the illness and increase the risk of suicidal behavior and suicide. Moreover, self-stigmatization undermines the person's ability to work toward his or her life goals and is a major obstacle in the rehabilitation and recovery process.

Family members of persons with mental illness may have stereotypes and prejudices about mental illness.

Alternatively, some persons with mental illness express righteous anger at stigmatization and discrimination, and develop behaviors to enhance self-empowerment. They seek to change the role of persons with mental illness in the mental health system by encouraging consumers to become participants in their treatment plans; by advocating for improvements in the quality of services; and by promoting more resource allocation and legislation for the mental health system. Still others are neither hurt nor driven by public stigma.

Unfortunately, feelings of shame, hiding and avoidance behaviors are common within the Israeli consumer community. Consumer advocacy organizations in Israel are rare, and within these organizations, there are few leaders willing to disclose themselves in the media or at a public event.

Family members of persons with mental illness may have stereotypes and prejudices about mental illness. Moreover, they may experience an associative stigma mechanism whereby the family unit is considered an extension of the person with mental illness. Another source of stigma and discrimination for the family is self-stigmatization. Some family members feel responsible for their child's, parent's, sibling's or mate's mental illness, and often experience self-blame, guilt and shame. Hence, the impact of public and self-stigma may be as harmful for family members as for the person with the mental illness.

A recent study of families of persons with mental illness in Israel found that they are stigmatized and discriminated against by the health care providers in their paternalistic attitudes and accusations; by the public's misunderstanding and lack of empathy; and by confusion and fear among friends and neighbors. Family members report feeling embarrassed about their close relative with a mental illness, and half of them blame themselves for having a role in the development of the illness. As a consequence, families can become isolated and withdraw from their social network. Parents, spouses and siblings report changes in their relationships with other members of their nuclear family.

Barriers to rehabilitation of persons with mental illness justify the need for anti-stigma campaigns and for adoption of anti-stigma and inclusion programmes in Israel.

Romania's Mentally Ill Are Treated with Brutality and Contempt

Erich Wiedemann

Erich Wiedemann is a journalist at the German newspaper Der Spiegel. *In the following viewpoint, he reports that conditions for the mentally ill in Romania are horrible. He focuses in particular on a mental asylum in Borsa. He says conditions there are filthy; patients often have only the clothes they are wearing and have little access to showers. He also asserts patients have little health care, though they are medicated heavily, often resulting in addiction. He says the government knows of the inhumane conditions, but stigma against the mentally ill is great, and there is no interest in improvement.*

As you read, consider the following questions:

1. Who is Paul-Otto Schmidt-Michel, and what is his relationship to the Borsa asylum?

2. What has the European Union done to try to improve the asylum, and has this been successful, according to Wiedemann?

3. Why does Wiedemann say that people in the area have resisted moving the asylum?

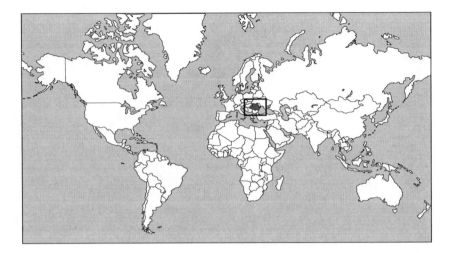

Doru discovered the dead man right after breakfast, lying in a meadow behind the lounge. A glass of water stood next to the charred corpse. The man had set himself on fire. Now he'll be examined by the doctors and then maybe he'll go to heaven, his friends say. He's put the worst behind him, they add.

Unwanted Outsiders

The other patients don't have that option. They have to put up with the stinking gray underworld of the mental asylum in the Romanian town of Borsa. None of them know if they will ever get out again—most of the patients in Borsa stay there until they die.

Mentally ill people are often seen as unwanted outsiders in Romania. No one wants to have to deal with them, and they're referred to colloquially as "varsa" ("weeds"). In this country, not even doctors believe a disturbed soul can become healthy again—once crazy, always crazy.

Borsa Castle is located in the most idyllic part of Transylvania, 260 kilometers (162 miles) west of Bucharest. It was the summer residence of the Bánffy family until shortly after the end of World War II. When the Communists threw the family out, Baroness Bánffy put a curse on the expropriated house, wishing for it to become an asylum. The reality was worse than her curse. Borsa Castle became one of the most monstrous mental institutions in Romania.

The annual death rate here is around 10 percent. Those patients who don't have relatives to bribe the attendants with food parcels and gifts can't afford to become seriously ill. If they do, they may end up rotting in their own feces.

Outside visitors aren't welcome in the castle—unless they're accompanied by Paul-Otto Schmidt-Michel, a professor of psychiatry from Ravensburg in western Germany who has become something of a godparent to the asylum.

In this country, not even doctors believe a disturbed soul can become healthy again—once crazy, always crazy.

Less than Rudimentary Care

A young man stands in front of the carved wooden gate to the dormitory building, holding an apple and babbling. His gaunt skull has been shaven, and he is wearing gray-striped pajamas and a brown bathrobe. On his right foot is a grubby sneaker, while his bare left foot is almost completely black. He holds the apple out to the visitors, saying "Bun venit" ("Welcome").

Outside the shack used for occupational therapy, patients assigned to the firewood detail are sawing logs. They are also dressed in pajamas and wearing plastic sandals.

Medical care here is as rudimentary as the clothing. During a visit last year [2005], Schmidt-Michel found a patient with a broken pelvis. "He had already been lying in bed, moaning with pain, for three days," he recalls. "No one took any notice of him. They said he was just pretending." The man would have died if Schmidt-Michel hadn't taken him to hospital.

"This way to the dormitories," says the attendant. He raises his index finger with a wink: Best not to touch anything. The clothes, pillows and mattresses here are infested with fleas and itch mites.

The stench is overwhelming. The asylum has only two showers—one for women, the other for men. According to regulations, every patient is supposed to shower once a week. But that's only possible when the well that supplies the asylum has enough water. In the summer, when the groundwater level sinks, the well often dries up for long periods. Then the lavatories become covered with excrement and the only washing machine doesn't work anymore. At these times, the patients often wear the same unwashed clothes for months.

Medical care here is as rudimentary as the clothing.

In the winter, the dormitories with their coal stoves are often not aired for weeks. There's no room to walk around in the dormitories, so many patients only leave their beds to eat or when they have to go to the toilet.

Around 40 patients are forced to share their beds with someone else, sleeping head-to-toe. During the cold season, they no longer see it as a problem, since they can keep each other warm.

There's little hope of the asylum's overcrowding getting better in the foreseeable future, because a bonus is paid for every new patient admitted. Schmidt-Michel tries to show understanding for the corrupt attendants and the director, Radu Ilea. Over the years, the staff members have lost their sensitivity to human suffering, he says, pointing out that the employees here are often struggling to survive themselves.

Passive Euthanasia

Schmidt-Michel says the conditions in some Romanian asylums have reminded him "of the treatment of mentally ill

Mental Health Services in Romania

Nationally, there are 908 psychiatrists (4.16 per 100,000 population), of whom 260 are child psychiatrists (1.19 per 100,000 population). They all work in the public health sector, although some also work in private ambulatory clinics. There are also psychologists and social workers in the mental health care system.

Most psychiatric services are provided by hospitals and outpatient clinics attached to the Ministry of Health. There are 38 psychiatric hospitals and many psychiatric departments in the general hospitals (a total of 17,079 beds) as well as day hospitals (1,222 beds) to care for patients with both acute and chronic mental illnesses; in addition there are 166 beds for patients with drug dependency. There are also 65 mental health centres for adults and children with mental illness. There are no private psychiatric hospitals.

The special needs of people with mental illness have not always been recognised and respected by the generic health services. However, a mental health law was passed in Romania only in August 2002. This was the first step towards reform of the mental health services and care system. . . . Only recently has Romania tried to add community mental health care services to the traditional system of active psychiatric hospital care. This started by radically reducing the number of beds, but unfortunately without ensuring adequate community care programmes and services. . . .

Stigma remains an obstacle in ensuring access to care for patients who are mentally ill. Stigma leads to the development of negative attitudes (including those of professionals), poor quality of treatment services and inadequate funding at both national and local level.

Nicoleta Tataru, "Romania," International Perspectives on Mental Health, *ed. Hamid Ghodse, London, UK: The Royal College of Psychiatrists, 2011, pp. 324–325.*

people under fascism." In Beclean on the Ukrainian border [in 1990], for example, . . . half of the 130 patients were kept in the cellar like animals. "That was passive euthanasia," he says.

Romania's transition to democracy hasn't changed anything in the country's mental asylums. In early 2004, it was reported that 17 patients in a hospital in Poiana Mare had died, most of them from hypothermia or undernourishment. When the state prosecutor's office investigated, it turned out that the death rate for 2004 was actually below average. More than 80 people had died in the institution the previous year, again mostly from starvation or cold.

The bureaucrats in Bucharest [the capital of Romania] are well informed about the misery in the country's mental asylums, but they're not doing anything about the situation. "That's to do with the state of ethical awareness here," Schmidt-Michel says.

The European Union [EU], which Romania will join on Jan. 1 [2007], isn't doing much either—even though the Romania's EU membership negotiations would have been a good opportunity to remind the government in Bucharest of its obligations towards the mentally ill. Simona Lupo from the department for social affairs at the EU's contact office in Bucharest says an action plan has been developed. "But we have to admit the situation hasn't improved that dramatically," she says. In other words, the situation is as bad as it was three years ago.

In Romania, the mental institutions are worse than the prisons. At least prison inmates can get a lawyer if they have the money, but for those in the psychiatric gulag there is no way to appeal.

Some patients in Borsa aren't even ill in the clinical sense. They're just being dumped here because they have no family or home, or because their spouses want to get rid of them. Sometimes people put their elderly parents in the asylum if there's no room for them in a nursing home.

Therapy is carried out almost entirely through medication, with the first tranquilizers already administered at breakfast time. Many of the patients only became ill because of the treatment they received here—anyone who takes two tranquilizers a day for years on end becomes addicted.

In Romania, the mental institutions are worse than the prisons.

The constant medication diminishes the mental and physical autonomy of the patients—which is clearly also the intention. The drugs administered in Romania's mental asylums are mostly haloperidol and levomepromazine, neuroleptics whose long-term use can cause movement disorders and damage to the central nervous system.

The Asylum Has Local Support

An attendant beats a hammer against a cast iron pipe outside the canteen—it's lunchtime. Today's meal is cabbage and potatoes in a thick sauce. Most patients sit on the grass and stare into space. Mentally handicapped and schizophrenic patients sometimes lose track of everything except their bodily functions and meal times.

The state of Romania pays four lei—just over €1 ($1.30)— per patient per day. Borsa has slightly better financial resources at its disposal than other asylums because Schmidt-Michel and a group of supporters from Ravensburg help out when money is tight. They also considered completely renovating the castle, but realized that it wasn't actually possible to repair the building. As a result, they are recommending that the mental asylum be moved to another location. Although the current location has few advantages, Schmidt-Michel's recommendations have provoked fierce resistance—mainly from the mayor and the local council. The clinic, after all, is the main employer in the area.

The farmers in the area also have an interest in the asylum staying in Borsa. They can hire those patients who are capable of work as day laborers to help out on their farms. Payment consists only of alcohol and cigarettes. Of course, alcohol is strictly prohibited in the asylum, but such infractions aren't punished.

"Borsa, what a hell you are," wrote Anja Hellstern, a nurse from the German city of Tübingen, in the diary she kept while she was doing her six months of voluntary social service here. And the attendants aren't the only offenders.

"It was the mute's washing day," she wrote. "Everything got lost in the bath except for his shoes and two ties. All his belongings were stolen by the criminals who were washing him. The poor boy cried and protested. There was nothing I could do, so I gave him a pair of socks. I got a smile in return."

In the United States, Mentally Ill Prisoners Face Inhumane Conditions

Human Rights Watch

Human Rights Watch (HRW) is an international human rights organization. In the following viewpoint, HRW argues that the mentally ill generally do not receive adequate treatment in US prisons. HRW points especially to the widespread use of solitary confinement in US prisons. HRW says that solitary confinement can exacerbate mental illness; in some cases, it can actually function as torture and cause trauma and mental illness in otherwise healthy patients. The organization recommends eliminating the widespread use of solitary confinement and also suggests significantly reducing the US prison population by discontinuing the imprisonment of people for nonviolent offenses. HRW asserts that without such changes, the United States is violating the human rights of mentally ill individuals in prison.

As you read, consider the following questions:

1. Why does HRW say that life in prison is particularly difficult for prisoners with mental illness?

2. What kinds of mental health services does HRW say are provided to prisoners in solitary confinement in "supermax" prisons?

Human Rights Watch, "Mental Illness, Human Rights, and US Prisons: Human Rights Watch Statement for the Record to the Senate Judiciary Committee Subcommittee on Human Rights and the Law," September 22, 2009. Reproduced by permission.

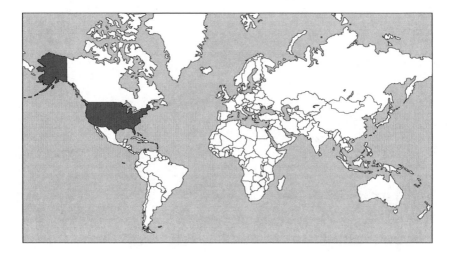

3. How does HRW believe that the Prison Litigation Reform Act should be modified?

Prisons were never designed as facilities for the mentally ill, yet that is one of their primary roles today. Many of the men and women who cannot get mental health treatment in the community [in the United States] are swept into the criminal justice system after they commit a crime. According to the Bureau of Justice Statistics, 56 percent of state prisoners and 45 percent of federal prisoners have symptoms or a recent history of mental health problems. Prisoners have rates of mental illness—including such serious disorders as schizophrenia, bipolar disorder, and major depression—that are two to four times higher than members of the general public. Studies and clinical experience consistently indicate that 8 to 19 percent of prisoners have psychiatric disorders that result in significant functional disabilities, and another 15 to 20 percent will require some form of psychiatric intervention during their incarceration.

Prison and Mental Illness

Mental health treatment can help some prisoners recover from their illness and for many others it can alleviate its painful symptoms, prevent deterioration, and protect them from suicide. It can enhance independent functioning and encourage the development of more effective internal controls. By helping individual prisoners regain health and improve coping skills, mental health treatment promotes safety and order within the prison environment and enhances community safety when prisoners are ultimately released.

Unfortunately, prisons are ill equipped to respond appropriately to the needs of prisoners with mental illness. Prison mental health services are all too frequently woefully deficient, crippled by understaffing, insufficient facilities, and limited programs. Many seriously ill prisoners receive little or no meaningful treatment.

Although there are many conscientious and committed mental health professionals working in corrections, they face daunting if not insurmountable challenges to meeting the needs of their patients: impossibly large case loads, physically unpleasant facilities, and institutional cultures that are unsympathetic to the importance of mental health services. Gains in mental health staffing, programs, and physical resources that were made in recent years have all too frequently since been swamped by the tsunami of prisoners with serious mental health needs. Overburdened staffs are hard-pressed to respond even to psychiatric emergencies, much less to promote recovery from serious illness and the enhancement of coping skills. Mindful of budget constraints and scant public support for investments in the treatment (as opposed to punishment) of prisoners, elected officials have been reluctant to provide the funds and leadership needed to ensure prisons have sufficient mental health resources. Twenty-two out of forty state correctional systems reported in a recent survey that they did not have an adequate number of mental health staff.

Without the necessary care, mentally ill prisoners suffer painful symptoms and their conditions can deteriorate. They are afflicted with delusions and hallucinations, debilitating fears, or extreme mood swings. They huddle silently in their cells, mumble incoherently, or yell incessantly. They refuse to obey orders or lash out without apparent provocation. They beat their heads against cell walls, smear themselves with feces, self-mutilate, and commit suicide.

Doing time in prison is hard for everyone. Prisoners struggle to maintain their self-respect and emotional equilibrium in facilities that are typically tense, overcrowded, fraught with the potential for violence, cut off from families and communities, and devoid of opportunities for meaningful education, work, or other productive activities. But life in prison is particularly difficult for prisoners with mental illnesses that impair their thinking, emotional responses, and ability to cope. They are more likely to be exploited and victimized by other prisoners. They are less likely to be able to adhere to the countless formal and informal rules of a strictly regimented life and often have higher rates of rule breaking than other prisoners.

"Supermax" Prisons and Isolation

When mentally ill prisoners break the rules, officials punish them as they would any other prisoner, even when their conduct reflects the impact of mental illness. If lesser sanctions do not curb the behavior, officials "segregate" the prisoners from the general prison population, placing them in super–maximum security ("supermax") prisons or in segregation units within regular prisons. Once isolated, continued misconduct—often connected to mental illness—can keep them there indefinitely. A disproportionate number of the prisoners in segregation are mentally ill.

Prison officials across the country have increasingly embraced long-term segregation to manage and/or to discipline prisoners who are perceived to be dangerous, but also those who are seen as difficult or disturbing. Supermax prisons such as Tamms Correctional Center in Illinois or segregation units in other prisons constitute the modern-day variant of solitary confinement. Prisoners are confined 23 to 24 hours a day in small cells that frequently have solid steel doors. They live with extensive surveillance and security controls; the absence of ordinary social interaction; abnormal environmental stimulus; a few hours a week of "recreation" alone in caged enclosures; and little, if any, educational, vocational, or other purposeful activities. They are handcuffed and frequently shackled every time they leave their cells.

Prolonged confinement under such conditions can be psychologically harmful to any prisoner, with the nature and severity of the impact depending on the individual, the duration, and the specific conditions (for example, access to natural light, radio, or books). It can provoke anxiety, depression, anger, cognitive disturbances, perceptual distortions, obsessive thoughts, paranoia, and psychosis. But the risk of harm is particularly grave for prisoners who already have serious mental illnesses. The stress, lack of meaningful social contact, and unstructured days can exacerbate symptoms of illness or provoke a reoccurrence. Suicides occur proportionately more often in segregation units than elsewhere in prison. All too frequently, mentally ill prisoners decompensate in isolation, requiring crisis care or psychiatric hospitalization. Many simply will not get better as long as they are isolated. According to one federal judge, putting mentally ill prisoners in isolated confinement "is the mental equivalent of putting an asthmatic in a place with little air. . . ." A recent story in the *Belleville News-Democrat* about Tamms profiled one prisoner with a well-documented history of paranoid schizophrenia who was held in solitary for nearly six years, mutilating himself and smearing feces. Other Tamms prisoners reportedly cut themselves, eat their own flesh, attempt suicide, and engage in other behaviors consistent with suffering from serious and untreated or poorly treated mental illness.

The psychological harm of super–maximum security confinement is exacerbated because mental health professionals are not permitted to provide a full range of mental health treatment services to the prisoners. Mental health services are typically limited to psychotropic medication, a health care clinician stopping at the cell front to ask how the prisoner is doing (that is, "mental health rounds"), and occasional meetings in private with a clinician. Individual therapy, group therapy, structured educational, recreational, or life-skill enhancing activities, and other therapeutic interventions are usually not available because of insufficient resources and clashes with prison rules—for example, insufficient numbers of custodial staff to take prisoners to and from their cells to private meetings with clinicians, and rules requiring prisoners to remain in their cells and prohibiting contact with other prisoners.

All too many mentally ill prisoners leave prison without arrangements to ensure they will continue to receive an appropriate level of mental health treatment.

In every class action challenging the placement of mentally ill prisoners in supermax confinement, plaintiffs have either won a court order or obtained a settlement prohibiting or greatly limiting such confinement. As a result, in prisons covered by the litigation, mentally ill prisoners are given more time out of their cells and greater access to mental health professionals and programs. Improved clinical responses of prisoners with mental illness in these prisons have been achieved without compromising safety or security. Unfortunately, except in the small number of prisons covered by this litigation, mentally ill prisoners continue to be sent to segregation; indeed, they are often disproportionately represented in segregation units.

Reentry to the Community

There is increasing awareness among public officials of the importance of providing reentry services to prisoners leaving prison as an effective means of increasing the likelihood they

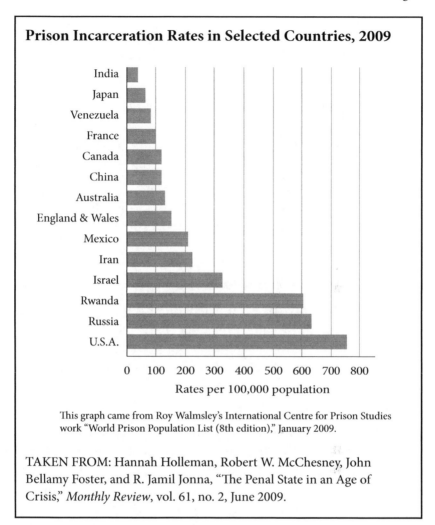

Prison Incarceration Rates in Selected Countries, 2009

Rates per 100,000 population

This graph came from Roy Walmsley's International Centre for Prison Studies work "World Prison Population List (8th edition)," January 2009.

TAKEN FROM: Hannah Holleman, Robert W. McChesney, John Bellamy Foster, and R. Jamil Jonna, "The Penal State in an Age of Crisis," *Monthly Review*, vol. 61, no. 2, June 2009.

will successfully make the transition back to the community. Men and women with mental illness have unique needs for discharge planning and reentry services. In addition to support for housing, employment, and income, they also need links to appropriate mental health treatment and access to public assistance. According to the Council of State Governments:

Individuals with mental illnesses leaving prison without sufficient supplies of medication, connections to mental health and other support services, and housing are almost certain to decompensate, which in turn will likely result in behavior that constitutes a technical violation of release conditions or new crimes.

Unfortunately, the need for reentry services far exceeds the supply. All too many mentally ill prisoners leave prison without arrangements to ensure they will continue to receive an appropriate level of mental health treatment, without ready access to public assistance, and without assistance to navigate the difficult waters of life after prison, in which the stigma of being a felon now accompanies all the problems that existed before incarceration.

A Human Rights Framework

Human rights standards acknowledge the unique vulnerability of prisoners to abuse and afford special protections to them. The UN [United Nations] Human Rights Committee has affirmed the "positive obligation" of states to protect the rights of those whose vulnerability arises from their status as persons deprived of their liberty.

Several discrete but interrelated human rights concepts are particularly relevant to the treatment of prisoners with mental illness: human dignity; the right to rehabilitation; the right to the highest attainable standard of health; and the right to freedom from torture or cruel, inhuman or degrading treatment or punishment. A prison operated within a human rights framework would provide a full range of mental health services with the staffing, resources, and facilities needed to serve the prison's population. Custodial policies and practices would be adjusted to ensure security and safety needs do not compromise mental health treatment. Staff would no longer constantly find themselves forced to choose between what they know they "should" be doing in terms of standards of care and sound principles of treatment, and what is feasible in the circumstances.

Respect for human rights of prisoners not only underpins and protects the fundamental values agreed on by the international community, it promotes safe and effective prison management. Unfortunately, human rights standards are all too often honored in the breach in US prisons. They are little known and almost never directly applied. . . .

"The prolonged isolation of detainees may amount to cruel, inhuman or degrading treatment or punishment."

Human Rights and Supermax Prisons

Human rights experts have long criticized prolonged solitary confinement, understood as physical isolation in a cell for 22 to 24 hours a day, such as exists in US supermax prisons. In 2008, the special rapporteur on torture concluded that "the prolonged isolation of detainees may amount to cruel, inhuman or degrading treatment or punishment, and, in certain instances, may amount to torture." Based on his research, he found that "the key adverse factor of solitary confinement is that socially and psychologically meaningful contact is reduced to the absolute minimum, to a point that is insufficient for most detainees to remain mentally well functioning." He stated that solitary confinement should only be used "in very exceptional cases" and "only as a last resort": the special rapporteur further noted that holding persons with mental illness in solitary confinement "cannot be justified for therapeutic reasons, or as a form of punishment." In 2007, the special rapporteur participated in the Fifth International Psychological Trauma Symposium held in Istanbul, Turkey, and with other prominent international experts produced a document titled "The Istanbul Statement on the Use and Effects of Solitary Confinement." Noting that solitary confinement "harms prisoners who were not previously mentally ill and tends to worsen the mental health of those who are," the Istanbul statement concludes that "solitary confinement should only be used in very exceptional cases, for as short a time as possible and only as a last resort." It should be "absolutely prohibited ... for mentally ill prisoners."

In 2006, the Human Rights Committee, reviewing US compliance with the ICCPR [International Covenant on Civil and Political Rights], stated that it

> reiterates its concern that conditions in some maximum security prisons are incompatible with the obligation contained in article 10 (1) of the covenant to treat detainees with humanity and respect for the inherent dignity of the human person. It is particularly concerned by the practice in some such institutions to hold detainees in prolonged cellular confinement, and to allow them out-of-cell recreation for only five hours per week, in general conditions of strict regimentation in a depersonalized environment. It is also concerned that such treatment cannot be reconciled with the requirement in article 10 (3) that the penitentiary system shall comprise treatment the essential aim of which shall be the reformation and social rehabilitation of prisoners. It also expresses concern about the reported high numbers of severely mentally ill persons in these prisons, as well as in regular U.S. jails.

Similarly, the Committee Against Torture on reviewing US compliance with CAT [referring to compliance with the Convention Against Torture and Other Cruel, Inhuman or Degrading Treatment or Punishment, also known as the Convention Against Torture] also expressed concern "about the extremely harsh regime imposed on detainees in 'super-maximum prisons'. The committee is concerned about the prolonged isolation periods detainees are subjected to, the effect such treatment has on their mental health, and that its purpose may be retribution, in which case it would constitute cruel, inhuman or degrading treatment or punishment."

Recommendations for Congress

Prescriptions for mental health care in prisons are plentiful. They are found in the standards and guidelines of the American Correctional Association and the National Commission on Correctional Health Care, in court rulings, expert reports, and in voluminous professional literature. What is lacking in prison mental health services is not knowledge about what to do, but the resources and commitment to do it. We hope the work of the subcommittee [referring to the Subcommittee on Human Rights and the Law of the Senate Judiciary Committee] will help marshal those resources and that commitment. Compassion, common sense, fiscal prudence, and respect for human rights dictate a better approach to the treatment of persons with mental illness in US prisons than is evident today.

The recommendations that follow focus on several key steps we believe Congress should take.

1. *Amend the Prison Litigation Reform Act (PLRA).* The Prison Litigation Reform Act of 1996 has placed serious obstacles in the path of prisoners seeking to protect their rights while incarcerated, including their rights to mental health treatment and services. One PLRA provision requires federal courts to dismiss prisoner lawsuits if prisoners have not exhausted the prison or jail grievance system. Prisoners with mental illness can find it impossible to comply with all the deadlines and technical rules in a grievance system, and may then find themselves forever barred from vindicating their rights in court. On the other hand, correctional agencies legitimately want a reasonable opportunity to respond to prisoners' complaints before having to defend themselves in court. Congress should amend the PLRA to remove the current exhaustion requirement and substitute a provision allowing courts to stay lawsuits temporarily to allow prisoners to take their complaints through the grievance system. Congress should also repeal the PLRA provision that denies compensation for "mental or emotional injury" absent a prior showing of physical injury.

Although isolated confinement and deficient mental health care can cause serious suffering and catastrophic injury to a prisoner's psychiatric condition, the PLRA's "physical injury" requirement bars a remedy for such injuries if the prisoner has not been physically injured as well. The Committee Against Torture called for repeal of the "physical injury" requirement when it last reviewed US compliance with the Convention Against Torture in 2006.

2. *Reduce High Incarceration Rates.* The United States has the highest rate of incarceration in the world because it puts so many people behind bars for low-level, nonviolent offenses and for lengthy periods of time. Prison should be reserved for dangerous or violent prisoners who must be securely confined; alternative sanctions should be used for low-level, nonviolent offenders. If prison populations were reduced there would be fewer persons with mental illness behind bars and more resources available for those who must be incarcerated. Congress should enact incentives to encourage states to reduce their prison populations and it should review federal laws to ensure federal prisons are not needlessly incarcerating low-level prisoners, including low-level drug offenders.

3. *Increase Funding for Mental Health Treatment in Prison.* Through the Mentally Ill Offender Treatment and Crime Reduction Act of 2004, which was reauthorized and extended for an additional five years in 2008, Congress has provided resources to state and local governments to design and implement collaborative initiatives between criminal justice and mental health systems that will improve access to effective treatment for people with mental illnesses involved with the justice system. To date, however, most of the funding awarded by the Bureau of Justice Assistance under the act has gone to either pre-

trial or post-release initiatives. Congress should ensure that federal funds are also used to improve the provision of mental health services to persons with mental disorders while they are incarcerated.

4. *Eliminate Prolonged Isolation of Mentally Ill Prisoners.* Congress should use its powers to protect prisoners with mental illness from being confined in the harsh isolation conditions typical of supermax prisons and other segregation or isolation units. It should directly instruct the [Federal] Bureau of Prisons (BOP) to end this harmful practice. It should also pass legislation precluding the awarding of federal funds for the construction or operation of any state prison or local jail if the jurisdiction has not instituted policies and practices to ensure mentally ill prisoners are not placed or kept in supermax prisons or other segregation units. Prisoners with mental illness who require extreme security precautions should be confined in specialized units that ensure human interaction and purposeful activities in addition to a full panoply of mental health services.

5. *Improve Correctional Mental Health Services.* In addition to increasing the flow of federal funds to support correctional mental health services provided by state and local jurisdictions, there are a number of other steps Congress could take to improve the treatment and conditions of confinement of prisoners with mental illness. . . .

6. *Improve Ex-Prisoner Access to Public Benefits Covering Mental Health Services.* Congress should secure changes to current laws and regulations in federal programs that fund mental health services that lead to delays in the restoration of eligibility for benefits for prisoners released from prison. Enabling ex-prisoners to receive Medicaid, Supplemental Security Income, and Social Security Disability Insurance immediately upon leaving

prison would enable them to pay for needed medication and mental health services in the community and to ensure continuity of care. Rapid restoration of benefits to released prisoners helps them manage their illness and reduces their risk of re-involvement with the criminal justice system.

Japan Imposes the Death Penalty on Mentally Ill Criminals

Amnesty International

Amnesty International (AI) is an international human rights organization. In the following viewpoint, AI argues that by international standards mentally ill people who cannot be held responsible for their actions should not be executed. AI says that Japan has executed a number of mentally ill prisoners or has kept them in harsh conditions awaiting execution. AI also says that Japan's prison system keeps those on death row in harsh conditions, is overly secretive, and otherwise violates international standards. AI recommends that Japan abolish the death penalty, or failing that, that it institute safeguards to prevent the execution of the mentally ill.

As you read, consider the following questions:

1. Why does Amnesty International call the use of the death penalty in Japan an anomaly?
2. According to the viewpoint, international human rights standards prohibit the imposition of the death penalty on what categories of people?

3. What recommendations does Amnesty International make to Japanese health professional bodies regarding mental illness and the death penalty?

In 2003 Mukai Shinji, who was reportedly suffering from mental health problems, was executed while his lawyer was preparing an appeal for a retrial.

On 23 August 2007 Japan executed three prisoners, including Takezawa Hifumi, born in 1937, who had reportedly been suffering from mental illness following a stroke, which made him paranoid and aggressive. According to reports of his trial, doctors acting for both the prosecution and the defence diagnosed Takezawa as mentally ill. However, he was deemed fully responsible by the court and sentenced to death.

Other Prisoners Executed

Other prisoners are reported to have been mentally ill prior to their execution. On 7 December 2007, Fujima Seiha and two other men were executed. He had earlier been found legally incompetent by the Supreme Court but had his sentence confirmed by the court in June 2004.

Miyazaki Tsutomu was convicted in 1997 of mutilating and killing four girls aged four to seven between 1988 and

1989. He was arrested in July 1989 after being caught molesting a girl. He reportedly showed no remorse for his crimes. He was given a range of psychiatric evaluations, and was diagnosed as suffering from dissociative identity disorder or schizophrenia. However, the Tokyo District Court judged that he was still aware of the gravity and consequences of his crimes and he was therefore accountable for them, sentencing him to death by hanging on 14 April 1997. His death sentence was upheld by the Tokyo High Court on 28 June 2001 and by the Supreme Court of Japan on 17 January 2006. After receiving psychiatric treatment for more than a decade, he was one of three inmates executed on 17 June 2008.

The effect of mental illness on the behaviour of an offender has long been recognized as a factor in determining culpability and appropriate punishment for crime. The application of the death penalty against prisoners who were "insane" at the time of their offence or who subsequently became insane has been prohibited for centuries in some jurisdictions. International human rights standards prohibit the imposition of the death penalty on, and the execution of, the mentally ill. This [viewpoint] examines the issue of mental health and the death penalty in Japan and is prompted by continuing reports of mentally ill prisoners in Japan being executed or detained in harsh conditions awaiting execution.

International human rights standards prohibit the imposition of the death penalty on, and the execution of, the mentally ill.

The challenges to researching the death penalty in Japan are considerable. The criminal justice system in Japan is secretive. Parliamentarians, legal reformers, national and international nongovernmental organizations (NGOs) and foreign politicians have all been refused access to death row or to see individual prisoners. Moreover, reliable information about individual prisoners' health is not readily available to their own lawyers—and certainly not directly from prison medical staff—and even family members of prisoners are uncertain about important aspects of their relative's health.

The Death Penalty in Japan— A Special Case

The use of the death penalty in Japan is an anomaly. The crime rate is low in comparison to other countries of a similar socioeconomic level of development and the number of murders is also low. The level of imprisonment is also relatively low. The number of prisoners convicted and sentenced to death is a small fraction of all those convicted of capital offences—a little over 1%. Nevertheless the imprisonment rate has risen over the past two decades, from 36 to 63 per 100,000 population and reflects and explains, in part, a perception that crime is rising. The press contribution to a discussion of capital punishment is predominantly limited to recounting the terrible impact of serious crimes such as murder; there is little public discussion on mental illness and crime; and there has been a surge in executions since 2006. (This surge reflects the increased willingness of recent ministers of justice who, under relevant legislation, must approve the execution of the condemned prisoner. Where a minister of justice opposes executions, none will take place.)

In a recent survey, Japan was one of only two Asian countries in which use of the death penalty was increasing and the only Asian country reported to show increasingly severe policies with respect to both the death penalty and imprisonment. Conditions in Japanese prisons are harsh and have been the subject for many years of criticism not only domestically but also by international NGOs and UN [United Nations] bodies. The situation in which death row prisoners find themselves is the harshest of all, with those suffering mental illness liable to suffer additional punishments because their behaviour is likely to infringe the draconian rules imposed on prisoners.

The Death Penalty, Mental Health, and Human Rights

At least since the adoption of the International Covenant on Civil and Political Rights (ICCPR) in 1966, the use of the death penalty has been seen in international human rights law as requiring restriction and control, with abolition seen as something to be encouraged in the short term and realized as soon as practicable. Subsequently there have been a number of international and regional standards applying to the death penalty. These included two statements from the UN Economic and Social Council restricting, inter alia [among other things], the use of the death penalty against people with mental disorders and resolutions of the former UN Commission on Human Rights calling for non-imposition and use of executions against people with mental disorders. The UN special rapporteur on extrajudicial, summary and arbitrary executions has affirmed the ban in international law on executing "mentally retarded or insane persons". In addition, a wide range of human rights organizations oppose the death penalty for different principled and practical reasons.

Amnesty International argues that the death penalty violates the right to life and the right not to be subjected to cruel, inhuman or degrading punishment. Amnesty International opposes the death penalty in all cases without exception regardless of the nature of the crime, the characteristics of the individual on whom it is imposed, and the method of execution used by the state. In practice the death penalty is applied arbitrarily—predominantly against marginalized populations. It is irreversible, it inflicts gross suffering on the condemned and on his or her loved ones, and no studies have demonstrated a unique deterrent effect of the death penalty.

It is widely recognized in criminal law and international human rights law that certain factors must be taken into consideration when an individual is tried, convicted and sentenced for a criminal act. While some factors might be aggravating—the level of violence used in the commission of a crime, for example—other facts are regarded as mitigating or even exculpatory, such as acting in self-defence or acting under the influence of a serious mental illness. Different national jurisdictions account for mitigating factors arising from mental status in different ways. Cases involving offenders with mental illness can give rise to verdicts of "not guilty due to insanity", "guilty but insane", and "guilty of manslaughter [rather than murder] due to diminished responsibility", among others. In cases where guilt is established by the court, the sentence may be lessened due to the mental state of the accused (though this is not always the case).

International human rights standards prohibit the imposition of the death penalty on certain categories of people (such as juvenile offenders, people with mental disabilities, the elderly, pregnant women and new mothers). In countries where the death penalty is retained in law and used, international law requires that the authorities prohibit and prevent the imposition of the death penalty and the execution of mentally ill prisoners.

Amnesty International argues that the death penalty violates the right to life and the right not to be subjected to cruel, inhuman or degrading punishment.

The widely shared proscription against executing the mentally ill reflects a general sense of unease at imposing the ultimate punishment on someone with limited understanding of, or diminished responsibility for, their actions. Moreover, such executions would fail key goals of punishment—retribution, reform, deterrence—with incapacitation being achieved only in the sense of extinguishing the life of the mentally ill person. For example, in the words of US Supreme Court justice Lewis Powell, the retributive function of the death penalty precludes execution of those "who are unaware of the punishment they are about to suffer and why they are to suffer it." This formed the basis for the ruling against executing the "insane" by the US Supreme Court in the case of *Ford v. Wainwright* in 1986.

Japan is not the only country failing to effectively prevent the imposition of the death sentence and the execution of the mentally ill. One observer of the US criminal justice system wrote of "the utter failure of the [US] criminal justice system to take adequate account of the effects of severe mental illness in capital cases, specifically by failing to assure a fair defence for defendants with mental disabilities, by failing to give morally appropriate mitigating effect to claims of diminished responsibility at the time of the crime, and by failing to correct these deficiencies in post-conviction proceedings." In a wider international setting, there is some evidence that mechanisms to evaluate and take into account the mental state of the prisoner in trial and appeal proceedings are inadequate.

Often the death penalty is imposed after unfair trials, and the conditions of detention experienced by prisoners under sentence of death frequently do not comply with international standards. Indeed on both counts, UN treaty monitoring bodies have expressed concerns at Japan's application of the death penalty. With regard to the conditions of detention there is an extensive array of human rights standards that, when applied to death row prisoners in Japan, would find Japan in breach. These include the International Covenant on Civil and Political Rights, the Standard Minimum Rules for the Treatment of Prisoners and the Body of Principles for the Protection of All Persons Under Any Form of Detention or Imprisonment. With regards to fair trial, there are serious concerns related to the overreliance on confessions obtained in police detention . . . , the lack of access to lawyers in private, and requests for retrial do not have the effect of staying the execution. The Human Rights Committee has raised specific issues with the government of Japan for more than a decade.

When Is Someone Sane Enough to Die?

Mental disorders can give rise to crimes, can be a contributing factor, or may not be directly relevant to the commission of a particular crime. It is the responsibility of the criminal justice system to take account of the mental state of the accused or convicted offender in order to meet both good penological practice [and] international human rights standards.

Moreover, these factors have to be taken account of at different stages of the judicial process. Mental disorders—including intellectual disability, delusions, hallucinations, depression—as well as temporary mental changes, such as those induced by forms of medication, alcohol or substances affecting mental state, may be relevant to the commission of a crime and the competence of the accused to stand trial; the capacity of the person to withdraw legal appeals; and the fitness of the prisoner to be executed. They may also be relevant in understanding the vulnerability of the accused to police interrogation and pressure to confess.

It is the responsibility of the criminal justice system to take account of the mental state of the accused or convicted offender in order to meet both good penological practice [and] international human rights standards.

In assessing these factors, courts frequently draw on the opinions of mental health professionals. However, the lines between mental health and mental illness, and between competence and lack of competence, are not fixed and different health professionals may come to different judgments. The fact that one possible outcome of these determinations could be the death of the prisoner adds considerable pressure to the assessment process.

In addition to assessments of mental state, mental health specialists may be called on to treat prisoners found incompetent, with the ultimate goal of such treatment possibly being the execution of the newly competent prisoner. Again this places the ethics of the health professionals concerned under pressure. The questions of assessing fitness for execution and restoration of competence by medical treatment are two ethical dilemmas that are faced by doctors as a consequence of the death penalty. Amnesty International believes that resolving these dilemmas can best be achieved by abolishing the death penalty and commuting all death sentences to terms of imprisonment. . . .

Key Recommendations

This [viewpoint] draws a number of conclusions and makes several recommendations for the government of Japan and to Japanese health professional bodies. The principal recommendations to government and to health professional organizations . . . are:

To government: Amnesty International's position on the death penalty is simple and widely known: It violates the right to life and it is the ultimate cruel, inhuman and degrading punishment. As such, Amnesty International campaigns for the abolition of the death penalty in all circumstances. Amnesty International calls on all states that retain the death penalty to establish a moratorium on executions during which it can set in place the consultative and practical measures required to abolish the death penalty in law. Irrespective of these measures, Amnesty International calls on governments to immediately reform laws and practices that conflict with international human rights standards as well as to give consideration to introducing reforms that will lead to better prison practice. In this spirit, Amnesty International calls on the government of Japan to address the issue of mental health and the death penalty by, inter alia, reviewing existing cases where mental illness may be a relevant factor, make all aspects of the death penalty more transparent, transfer responsibility for prisoner health to the Ministry of Health, Labour [and Welfare], end the lack of notice of execution to prisoners and their families, and improve conditions for prisoners under sentence of death. . . .

To Japanese health professional bodies: Amnesty International calls on Japanese medical, psychiatric, and nursing associations to ensure they have clearly stated positions against professional participation in capital punishment; promote good prison health care on an ethical basis; and ensure that prison health care is subject to external transparent review and accountability.

In China, the Mental Health System Is Used to Silence Political Dissent

Wan Yanhai

Wan Yanhai is a Chinese AIDS activist, doctor, and worker for public health; he moved to America in 2010 because of persecution by the Chinese government. In the following viewpoint, Wan says that mental illness is poorly understood in China and that the mentally ill often do not receive proper treatment. On the other hand, he says, many people who are seen as a threat to the state—dissidents, gays, lesbians, and members of religious groups such as Falun Gong—may be diagnosed as mentally ill and placed in institutions to silence them. Wan says it is important to publicize such abuses in order to promote change.

As you read, consider the following questions:

1. Who is Xu Lindong, and what does the author say happened to him?
2. What is the Beijing Aizhixing Institute of Health Education, and how does the author describe its mission?
3. In Beijing, what government departments operate mental hospitals, and why does the author believe that this is a problem?

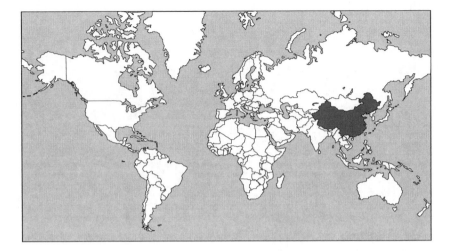

According to a 2009 article in the British medical journal the *Lancet*, as many as 17.5 percent of China's adult population may suffer from some kind of mental illness. Yet mental health remains a vexing, and in some cases taboo, topic in China. The trauma and reversals of recent decades, from the Cultural Revolution [a government-sponsored terror from 1966–1976] to the current all-consuming drive for wealth, from shifting family structures to the migration of millions of people each year from villages to cities to find work, all have put invisible strains on the people living through these vast changes. Some recent headlines from the past year [2010] indicate that untreated mental illness may be becoming a more acute problem in China: a series of grisly attacks by middle-aged men on schoolchildren, some of them deadly, caused a great public panic. The suicides of several young workers at a factory in southern China assembling iPhones likewise raised questions about where migrants (most workers are living far from home) can turn to for emotional support in difficult times.

Medicine as a State Weapon

Meanwhile, even as many people who need medical attention are unable to receive help—either because it is too costly or because of the great social stigma attached—there are others who are healthy but are labeled "mentally ill" by authorities seeking a reason to detain them in mental health hospitals, as the *New York Times* recently documented. One man mentioned in the article, for instance, is 54-year-old Xu Lindong, who was forced to spend six and a half years in mental hospitals and subjected to 54 electric-shock treatments following a land dispute. (A recent *New Yorker* article explored the interest—and confusion—among some in China regarding the ideas of [psychoanalyst] Sigmund Freud.) This is the tragic irony of mental health in China today: Many whose lives could be improved will never receive medical attention, and many who don't need it are held in confinement in the name of medicine.

In this context, I would like to offer my own personal story. I was trained in medicine in the 1980s and subsequently worked for a government health institute and then for a private NGO [nongovernmental organization] dedicated to AIDS awareness, which brought me into contact with marginalized populations and stigmatized people in China, including those wrongly labeled as mentally ill. I have seen people sent to mental hospitals for being gay, for domestic disputes, and for political dissent.

I was born in 1963 and grew up in a small town in Anhui province. The first person I remember being described as mentally ill was my father. He was a police officer in the 1950s; he found his work very hard to do, and by the time he left his job in the late 1950s, he hated politics. During the Cultural Revolution, which began in 1966 and lasted for 10 years, he spent time in a labor camp. There were two words people used during my childhood to describe people with a mental illness: One was *fengzi*, which means a dangerous person without restraint or a conscience. The other was *naozi shou ciji*, which means someone with a mind broken by pain or stress. That was what they said of my father. He was not ever formally diagnosed because there was very little understanding of mental health at that time in China; under Mao Zedong [authoritarian leader of Communist China from 1949–1976], it was seen as a sign of weakness. I think my father's problem was not mental illness, but instead that he had an independent mind. He read a lot and thought differently about the world. In the 1970s, people often used the label of mental illness for people like that.

Many whose lives could be improved will never receive medical attention, and many who don't need it are held in confinement in the name of medicine.

Some Progress Is Made

In secondary school, I had to decide between focusing on science or on politics and literature. My father said to me, "If you study politics and literature, you will have to lie. But if you study science, it has nothing to do with politics." He also made the argument: "Even if you are put in prison, the police will be kinder to you if you are a doctor." After the Cultural Revolution, many families encouraged their children to study science, engineering, and medicine. That is how I came to attend Shanghai First Medical College, which I entered in 1981.

During that time, interest in Western notions of mental illness grew quickly. The 1980s were a period of relative openness in China, when foreign ideas on everything from art to politics to medicine to environmentalism began to flood into China. During the Cultural Revolution, psychology was considered a "pseudo-science." But after 1986, I remember a lot of lectures at university on psychology and psychoanalysis. In 1987, I helped to translate two chapters from an English-language book about psychological counseling and crisis intervention. I graduated in 1988 and moved to Beijing, where I got a job as a health researcher for the National Health Education Institute, which is part of the Ministry of Health. I remember in 1989 when the ministry established the first suicide-prevention hotline in Beijing. By no means did Chinese health professionals understand or accept mental health issues the way Westerners did in those years. Still, the trend was clearly toward a more progressive understanding, focused on improving the lives of patients.

In 1995, I founded one of China's first NGOs, the [Beijing] Aizhixing Institute of Health Education, with a mission of increasing awareness, treatment, and prevention efforts for HIV/ AIDS in China. My work brought me into contact with some of the sub-populations most affected by the disease, including gays and lesbians, drug users, and sex workers. All suffer great social stigma in China. Until 2000, being gay was technically classified as a mental illness in China, but gay people still suffer extraordinary discrimination. I remember in 1997, when a 30-something lesbian woman attended a meeting held by Aizhixing on lesbian rights. She was quick and energetic. She told me her family had sent her to a mental hospital for six months because she was not married and they thought something must be wrong. She asked me, "Was this the right approach?" Of course I told her it was not. We talked about the confusion on the hushed topic of sexuality and mental illness.

Hospitalizing the Healthy

In the past 10 years, I believe that an increasing number of healthy people have been hospitalized as "mentally ill." This is troubling to me. The trend began with the government crackdown on the dissident religious group Falun Gong, which was banned in 1999. The authorities labeled members of the group as mentally ill—and therefore an alleged threat to social stability—and used that as pretense to confine them. When the government saw that approach could be useful, it expanded the strategy to target a broad swath of political dissidents and petitioners.

Falun Gong

Falun Gong ... is a Chinese spiritual movement founded in 1992 by Li Hongzhi (1951–). Although most Western scholars would classify it as a "new religious movement," Li and his followers understand Falun Gong not as a religion but as a "cultivation system," based on principles of *qigong* that are widely accepted in China. Falun Gong rapidly became very popular in China, attracting millions of followers in the years immediately after its founding. For complex reasons, Falun Gong soon ran afoul of the Chinese state, and a massive protest in Beijing by Falun Gong practitioners against media censure at the end of April 1999 led to a harsh crackdown by the Chinese government on the grounds that Falun Gong was a dangerous "heterodox sect."

David Ownby, *"Falun Gong,"*
Encyclopedia of Religion, *ed. Lindsay Jones,*
Detroit, MI: Macmillan Reference USA, *2004, p. 2978.*

Because of my own work on the controversial topic of AIDS, I have been detained three times, and in May 2010 I left China because of increasing political pressure. I have crossed paths with many activists and NGO leaders in similar positions; we all want to improve the lives of people in China, but the government finds our work threatening. We did not form organizations to be against the Chinese government, but we are sometimes considered by the officials to be dissidents or troublemakers. One example is Zhou Yi Juan, a Buddhist nun who in 2005 organized a memorial in Tiananmen Square to the victims of the June 4, 1989, massacre. Afterward, she was forced to enter a mental hospital for psychiatric treatment. In 2007, Aizhixing supported her with a fellowship to write a memoir about this experience; two years later, she took legal action and sued the hospital. I believe that these cases should be known more widely.

Today in Beijing three government branches operate mental hospitals: the health department, the police department, and the civil affairs department. This is troubling evidence that mental health is not seen as a medical issue, as it should be, but as a matter of social stability and a concern of law enforcement. This attitude leads to abuses, and there is no appeal process for people like Zhou Yi Juan. In Zhejiang province, an official document dated March 23, 2010, and published online details the collaboration between the local police and health departments on mental health, which is wrongly described as first and foremost a social stability issue. In a troubling return to the climate of suspicion my parents experienced during the Cultural Revolution, neighbors in Zhejiang are encouraged to report on each other if they suspect mental illness.

These examples represent only a small glimpse of the vast confusion over mental health in China. These are tragedies the world should know about. The impulse to hide the problems is the worst approach.

In Russia, the Mental Health System May Be Used to Silence Political Dissent

Yuri Savenko, as told to Vaughan Bell

Yuri Savenko is president of the Independent Psychiatric Association of Russia (IPA); Vaughan Bell is a clinical and research psychologist who works for Médecins Sans Frontières as mental health lead for Colombia. In the following viewpoint, Bell notes that under the Soviet Union, psychiatry was often used to institutionalize and intimidate dissidents. He worries that Russia today is using some of the same methods. Savenko confirms that modern-day Russia is using psychiatric institutions as an arm of the state and is institutionalizing those it sees as enemies of the government. Savenko says that Western countries can help the situation in Russia by speaking out against the use of psychiatry for political purposes.

As you read, consider the following questions:

1. What is the difference between the Independent Psychiatric Association of Russia and the All-Union Society of Psychiatrists and Narcologists?

2. According to Savenko, on what grounds were Larisa Arap and others hospitalized, and why was this unjust?

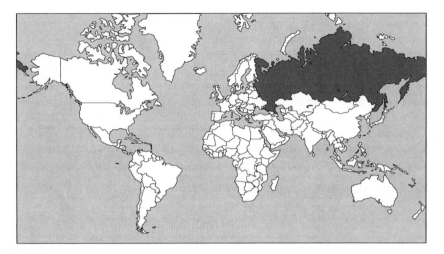

3. What are two examples Savenko gives of positive developments in Russia's mental health system?

Recent Western press reports have indicated that the Russian psychiatric system might be experiencing a return to the 'bad old days' when it was used in part to suppress political dissidents.

History of Abuse

President of the human rights focused psychiatrists' organization the Independent Psychiatric Association of Russia (IPA), Dr Yuri Savenko, has kindly agreed to talk to Mind Hacks [the website that published this interview] about the current situation.

In 1983 the main Russian psychiatric association, the All-Union Society of Psychiatrists and Narcologists, resigned from the World Psychiatric Association [WPA] before it could be expelled.

While the society claimed it was being 'slandered', evidence was presented to the WPA of high-profile dissidents being sent to psychiatric hospitals on the basis of their political beliefs.

At the end of the 1980s, the Independent Psychiatric Association of Russia was formed by psychiatrists and health professionals wanting to expose abuses in the system and provide an alternative to the existing professional organisation. They gained independent admission to the WPA in 1989.

Recent press reports have suggested that both people who fall foul of criminals and high-profile dissidents have been subject to 'punitive psychiatry.'

As the Soviet Union became more open in the period of Glasnost [openness] reforms [during the late 1980s] a delegation of American psychiatrists were invited to assess Soviet psychiatric facilities in 1989 and reported significant evidence that political dissidents had been subjected to "excessive and inappropriate" detainment and treatment.

This spurred a reform in Russian psychiatry and after much debate the All-Union Society of Psychiatrists and Narcologists were readmitted to the WPA, leading to new hopes for a renewed Russian psychiatric system and, indeed, further revelations about past abuses.

However, recent press reports have suggested that both people who fall foul of criminals and high-profile dissidents have been subject to 'punitive psychiatry', suggesting a return to the dark days of Soviet psychiatry and 'psikhuska' [psychiatric prison] hospitals.

The case of journalist Larisa Arap has been of particular concern recently, after she was admitted to a psychiatric hospital and forcibly medicated after she wrote about alleged abuses in the same clinic only weeks earlier. Her friends and relatives protested that she showed no evidence of mental illness.

IPA president and psychiatrist Dr Yuri Savenko agreed to give his views on the current situation in Russia.

Note: Dr Yavenko answered the questions in Russian which were translated into English by an IPA member. The translation is left unaltered. . . .

Punitive Psychiatry

[Mind Hacks:] *What evidence is there that people are currently being subjected to "punitive psychiatry" in Russia?*

[Dr Yavenko:] Such tendency does exist and the Independent Psychiatric Association of Russia has been working on this issue for the past 18 years. Since 1995, regardless of the protest of Russian psychiatric society, psychiatry became a tool to close religious organizations. This method quickly became a routine and led to corruption as well as the loss of independent judicial powers.

From 1997, members of the IPA were also not allowed to take any part in the forensic psychiatric [that is, psychiatry related to law] examination commission of the Serbsky Center [the main center for forensic psychiatry in Russia] even though it was never officially ruled. In addition, the Serbsky Center legitimized their actions and this evolved into a total state control of the forensic psychiatric evaluation. Therefore, no outside party could be a part of the expertise commission.

With the introduction of the new "extremism" law, which is considered as rather vague, we find ourselves retreating back to the Soviet times. The law is very broad and any form of criticism against the state or public institutions may be considered as "extremism". It's just the same situation as we had in Soviet times with the former law article of "slandering of the Soviet powers" and cases handled by the authority. Therefore, it is not surprising that over the years, the number of unsatisfied Russian citizens who had once crossed paths with the authority, has soared.

Many of them are sent to forensic psychiatric evaluation. They often are members of human rights groups and civic society organizations. Although these members are usually qualified by psychiatrists adequately, they would not have been examined by psychiatrists if not for the distaste for the article mentioned above. In addition, we have also been confronted with an abuse of legal regulations, specifically pertaining to the widening of the medical term, "danger or threat to the public."

With the introduction of the new "extremism" law . . . we find ourselves retreating back to the Soviet times.

With respect to the cases of Larisa Arap from Murmansk, Olga Popova in Moscow, Andrei Novinka from Rybinsk and others, people were hospitalized under the pretense of being a "danger to the public," when in fact, not one of these cases showed any signs [of] aggression, danger or threat. This example shows that people with mental disorders are the most vulnerable group of population; they become the first victims of politicization of society and the first indicators of critical levels of such politicization.

Political Influence

What reasons might people be subject to unjustified psychiatric treatment?

This is the most convenient way to make opposition keep silence, to intimidate it, more over that there is unforgotten experience of such actions. The newly formulated articles of the laws of "extreme measure" and "maltreatment of people of different ethnicity and race" is a continuation of the old system in the Soviet times. The first victims are critics of authority, public protesters, people who often apply to court, etc.

Newspaper reports have suggested that some of the alleged cases have been politically motivated. Is there evidence of systematic political influence on the psychiatric system or on individual clinicians?

Everything in politically oriented society takes on political sound, especially—as it was in the case of Larisa Arap—when it draws the attention of international society. Any criticism of the state power and any grafts of "orange opposition" [1] are considered as political danger.

This is the most convenient way to make opposition keep silence, to intimidate it.

This will then have an effect on the psychiatric services and the work of doctors. The professional public is frightened by the authoritative atmosphere in the country and it is difficult to find a professional willing to stand in the opposition of the powers.

What action can be taken against clinicians who abuse their position?

Theoretically, professional society can express censure on them, they can be deprived of medical diploma or find themselves under criminal prosecution, but in the end, doctors generally tend to go unpunished.

What needs to be done to improve Russian psychiatry?

Other democratic countries could play an important role in developing proper use of psychiatry in Russia under the conditions that:

1. Russia must adhere to the international conventions and recommendations on psychiatric health and Russia's actions must be supervised under a special commission.

2. It's necessary to demonstrate to the main supporters of punitive psychiatry in Russia, first of all, administration of the Serbsky Center . . . inadmissibility of their position, to force them to make appropriate statements.

3. All Russian psychiatric organizations must stress on maintaining equal relationship with one another.

1. The Orange Revolution was a series of 2004 protests in Russia's neighbor, Ukraine.

What are the positive developments in the Russian mental health system?

Positive changes in the Russian mental health system consist of:

1. The adoption of the law: On psychiatric care and guarantees of citizens' rights in its provision.

2. Negotiating a separation from the universal psychiatry.

3. The formation of a human rights–oriented psychiatric organization, the Independent Psychiatric Association of Russia (a member of the World Psychiatric Association since 1989).

4. There are a greater number of medical and psychotherapeutic resources available to improve the rehabilitation of the mentally ill.

Update: I e-mailed Dr Valery Krasnov, president of the Russian Society of Psychiatrists, to request a commentary on this [viewpoint] but received no response.

Periodical and Internet Sources Bibliography

The following articles have been selected to supplement the diverse views presented in this chapter.

BBC News	"Japan Death Row 'Breeds Insanity,'" September 10, 2009.
Emilia Chiscop	"A Dive into the Romanian Mental Health System: What Lies Behind Some Horrors," Carter Center, December 16, 2008. www.cartercenter.org.
Zofeen Ebrahim	"Pakistan: Mental Illness Among Women: Gender-Driven?," Inter Press Service, January 31, 2010. http://ipsnews.net.
Tanya Greene	"ACLU to United Nations: Solitary Confinement Violates Human Rights," *Blog of Rights*, March 5, 2012. www.aclu.org.
Abdi Guled	"Kept in Chains: Mental Illness Rampant in Somalia," Phys.org, May 20, 2011.
Human Rights Europe	"Inhuman and Degrading Conditions in Romanian Psychiatric Hospital," March 14, 2012. www.humanrightseurope.org.
Lancet	"Execution of Prisoners with Mental Illnesses in Japan," vol. 374, no. 969, September 12, 2009.
Calum MacLeod	"Chinese Citizens Sent to Mental Hospitals to Quiet Dissent," *USA Today*, December 29, 2011.
Jeffrey L. Metzner and Jamie Fellner	"Solitary Confinement and Mental Illness in U.S. Prisons: A Challenge for Medical Ethics," *Journal of the American Academy of Psychiatry and the Law*, vol. 38, no. 1, March 2010.
Graham Thornicroft, Diana Rose, and Nisha Mehta	"Discrimination Against People with Mental Illness: What Can Psychiatrists Do?," *Advances in Psychiatric Treatment*, vol. 16, 2010.

CHAPTER 3

Mental Illness and
Substance Abuse

Alcohol Use and Mental Health in Developing Countries

Vikram Patel

Vikram Patel is senior research fellow in clinical science at the Wellcome Trust and joint director of the Centre for Global Mental Health. In the following viewpoint, he asserts that mental health resources are inadequate in most developing countries. He also says that alcohol consumption rates in these countries are not high but that drinking patterns, especially among men, can be dangerous. He argues that there is not much research linking mental illness and alcoholism in developing countries, but he cites a number of studies showing alcohol use linked to stress, suicide, and other mental health conditions. Patel concludes that more research must be done on the relationship between alcohol use and mental health in developing countries.

As you read, consider the following questions:

1. How does Patel say the profile of mental health in developing countries is increasing?

2. According to Patel, how does the importance of male sexuality help shape drinking patterns in some cultures?

3. What evidence does Patel provide of links between alcohol consumption and suicide rates in developing countries?

This paper provides an overview of mental health and alcohol use in developing countries. The review shows that mental disorders are common and pose a significant burden on the health of developing nations. There are close associations between poor mental health and other public health and social development priorities. Although the overall use of alcohol at the population level is relatively low, with high abstention rate, drinking patterns among those who do drink are often hazardous. The consumption of alcohol is heavily gendered and is characterized by a high proportion of hazardous drinking among men. Hazardous drinkers do not only consume large amounts of alcohol, but also do so in high-risk patterns, such as drinking alone and bingeing. Hazardous drinking is associated with depressive and anxiety disorders as well as suicide and domestic violence. The limited evidence base suggests that moderate or casual drinking is not associated with social or health hazards; any likely benefits of moderate drinking for mental health have not been studied in developing countries. The implications of this evidence base for future research and policy are discussed.

Ann Epidemiol 2007;17:S87–S92.

KEY WORDS: Mental Health, Developing Countries, Alcohol Abuse, Comorbidity.

Introduction

This paper assesses evidence of mental health harm and benefits associated with drinking alcohol in the context of developing countries. Developing countries, categorized as low or middle income in the World Bank's classification, account for more than 80% of the world's population and, unsurprisingly, are home to the majority of individuals living with mental disorders.

This paper has 4 parts: It provides an overview of mental health in developing countries, reviews what we know about drinking patterns and their correlates in these countries, considers the evidence on the relationship between drinking and mental health, and suggests implications for policy and future research.

Research for this article has been derived from two major sources:

- A search of MEDLINE and PsycInfo databases, using the following search terms: alcohol* AND (psycholo* OR psychiatr* OR mental* health OR mental* disorder*) AND develop* countr*; and alcohol* AND (psycholo* OR psychiatr* OR mental* health OR mental* disorder*) AND (Africa* OR Asia* OR South America*); for the period 1996 to date

- A hand search of books and chapters pertaining to alcohol use in developing countries, in particular two publications from the World Health Organization (WHO) (1, 2)

Selected abbreviations and acronyms:

DALY = disability-adjusted life years

HIV/AIDS = Human Immunodeficiency Virus/Acquired Immunodeficiency Syndrome

ICD-10 = *International Statistical Classification of Diseases and Related Health Problems, 10th Revision*

MDG(s) = Millennium Development Goal(s)

WHO = World Health Organization

YLD = years lived with disability

Mental Health in Developing Countries

At any given time, about 10% of the adult population globally and about one in three adults attending a primary health center suffers from a mental disorder. Depression and anxiety (the "common mental disorders") and alcohol and drug abuse (the "substance abuse disorders") are the most frequent of all mental disorders. Psychotic disorders, such as schizophrenia and bipolar disorder, although relatively less common, are profoundly disabling. It is no surprise that mental disorders figure prominently in the list of leading global causes of disability (see Table 1 [not shown]) (3, 4). The burden is the greatest during the most productive years of life—young adulthood—when about 75% of all mental disorders seen in adults begin (5). Among people aged 10 to 59 years in developing countries, four conditions linked to mental health and alcohol abuse can be found in the 10 leading causes of death (road traffic accidents, self-inflicted injuries, violence, and cirrhosis of the liver) (4). If disease burden is measured through the number of years lived with disability (YLD), then unipolar depressive disorders is the leading contributor to disease burden in developing countries; schizophrenia and alcohol abuse disorders also figure in the leading 10 causes of YLD (4) (Table 1). Altogether, neuropsychiatric disorders account for 9.1% of disability-adjusted life years (DALYs) in low-income countries and 17.7% of DALYs in middle-income countries.

The enormous gap between mental health needs and services in developing countries has been addressed in a series of high-profile international documents, culminating in the 2001 "World Health Report" (3) and the WHO "Mental Health Atlas" (6). Of the 400 million people with mental disorders, most live in developing countries. Meanwhile, more than 90% of global mental health resources are concentrated in rich countries. In many developing countries, for example, there is about one psychiatrist for every million people (6). As a result, the majority of individuals suffering from mental disorders do not seek professional help, and families bear the brunt of the untreated morbidity and disability.

Formal health care in developing countries often takes the form of primary and traditional medical care. In primary care, mental disorders typically go undetected, with patients receiving a cocktail of treatments targeting the various symptoms of mental disorders—for example, sleeping pills for sleep problems and vitamins for fatigue (7). Psychosocial treatments are rarely provided. Often, only persons with psychotic disorders with disturbed behavior are brought to specialist mental health services (if these are available). In such establishments, care is heavily biased toward drug therapies. Mental illness is strongly associated with stigma (8); human rights violations and institutionalization characterize services for severe mental disorders (9).

At any given time, about 10% of the adult population globally ... suffers from a mental disorder.

At the same time, the profile of mental health in developing countries is increasing. More governments are designing and implementing mental health policies (4); more donors are supporting mental health–related work; more public health professionals and policy makers are taking an interest in mental health issues. The pace of reform is slow, however. With every new challenge to the public health sector, mental health is relegated to the shadows.

Thus mental health is absent from the United Nations Millennium Development Goals (MDGs), which set out a vision for development with a focus on health and education (see Table 2 [not shown]) (10, 11), despite the close link of mental health with many of the individual MDGs (12). For instance, a major reason why children are not able to either enroll in schools or complete primary education (MDG 2) is related to their developmental and mental health (e.g., due to various types of learning disabilities). Depression is one of the most common health problems affecting women during pregnancy (MDG 5) and after childbirth; depression during motherhood is associated with low birth weight and infant failure to thrive, both of which are linked to infant mortality (MDG 4) (13, 14). There are several areas of confluence between HIV/AIDS (MDG 6) and mental health: people with mental health problems, particularly alcohol use disorders, are at greater risk for HIV/AIDS; individuals with HIV/AIDS are more likely to suffer mental health problems, and these problems, in turn, can affect their overall health outcomes (15). In general, virtually all population-based studies of the risk factors for mental disorders—particularly, for depressive and anxiety disorders and substance abuse disorders—show higher prevalence among the poor and marginalized. Mental disorders impoverish people through the costs of health care and as a result of lost employment opportunities (16). Treatment, thus, may help people rise out of poverty (MDG 1).

For many years, we lacked evidence that anything could be done for mental disorders in poor countries. However, a number of clinical trials have been published recently from across the developing world, demonstrating the efficacy and cost-effectiveness of locally feasible treatments for depression, schizophrenia, and substance abuse. Studies have demonstrated that community care for schizophrenia is feasible and leads to superior clinical and disability outcomes (17). Both antidepressant and psychosocial treatments are efficacious for depression (18). Community initiatives reduce the rates of substance abuse disorders (19). Perhaps the best examples that management of suffering is possible derive not from trials, but from the remarkable work of grassroots organizations implementing mental health interventions (20).

Alcohol Use in Developing Countries

The pattern of alcohol use in many developing countries is closely linked to three broad historical phases. The preindustrial, precolonial phase was characterized by traditional alcohol consumption, often within the context of specific culturally sanctioned events (such as religious ceremonies). Records of the use of traditional alcohols, brewed from locally grown grains, vegetables, or fruits, can be found in the majority of developing countries. The second phase was associated with the advent of colonial rule that affected vast regions of the developing world. The colonial rulers from Europe brought with them distilled alcohols and beer, native to their own cultures. The introduction of these foreign beverages led to new legislations in some countries regarding taxation and the consumption of alcohol. Traditional alcohols continued to be widely used but remained outside the tax net and concern of the colonists; European alcohols were more expensive than local drinks and were mainly consumed by the colonists and the more affluent sections of the local community. The third historical phase coincides with the postcolonial period. In many developing countries, it has been characterized by globalization of economic markets and the increasing availability of international brands of distilled alcohols.

Today, distilled alcohols are freely available in many developing countries and include both local and international brands. Significant variations exist in patterns of drinking between—and within—countries in terms of the proportion of total drinking accounted for by traditional and distilled alcohols. As a general rule, however, distilled alcohols and wine are generally consumed by more urban and affluent groups, while traditional alcohols (such as sorghum-based beer and palm wine in Africa) are consumed by more rural and poorer populations; beer seems to be popular across the social classes. In addition, in many societies, traditional beverages are more popular among older drinkers, while distilled malt and barley-based beers are preferred by younger generations and those with "more European or American cultural orientation" (1, p. 22). There is considerable variation in the age of initiation of drinking. In many tribal societies, this may take place relatively early, but typically in the context of a traditional ritual (as opposed to drinking for pleasure, as in developed countries).

Table 3. Median per Capita Consumption of Alcohol per Adult 15 Years of Age and Over, by WHO Geographical Region

| | Consumption L | | Countries with survey data/total number | Percent of population |
Region	Mean	Median	of countries	covered
AFRO	1.37	0.95	28/46	76.72
AMRO	6.98	5.74	32/35	99.96
EMRO	0.30	0.53	12/21	90.33
EURO	8.60	8.26	49/52	99.99
SEARO	1.15	0.99	7/11	98.38
WPRO	5.54	1.95	20/27	99.94

Modified from World Health Organization 35, World Health Organization 1.
L = Liters. AFRO = African; AMRO = Americas; EMRO = Eastern Mediterranean; EURO = Europe; SEARO = Southeast Asia; WPRO = Western Pacific.

TAKEN FROM: Vikram Patel, "Alcohol Use and Mental Health in Developing Countries," *Annals of Epidemiology*, vol. 17, no. 5S, May 2007, p. S89.

A number of studies address the prevalence of alcohol use and alcohol use disorders in developing countries (e.g., 1, 2). However, there is wide variation in the study methods used, including how alcohol use and various disorders are defined, as well as in the sampling strategies. These variations make comparisons difficult. Typically, surveys target populations considered to be at high risk (e.g., young people), individuals in primary health care, or those in psychiatric facilities. The recently completed World Health Surveys will provide a global picture of alcohol use and its association with socioeconomic and health factors. Meanwhile, a number of findings can be discerned from the existing literature.

First, per capita alcohol consumption is relatively low in developing countries (see Table 3) with the lowest rates reported in Africa, Southeast Asia, and the Middle East. This, in part, attests to the heavy influence of social, cultural, and economic factors on alcohol use. In comparison with developed countries, a much smaller proportion of population—in particular, among women—consumes alcohol in developing countries.

Second, alcohol use and alcohol use disorders are more prevalent in men than in women across regions, with gender gaps particularly wide in developing countries. It is likely that both psychosocial and biological etiologies converge to lead to the greater risk of alcohol use disorders in men. In many countries, drinking and intoxication among men are more socially acceptable than among women and may have important social meanings, such as maintaining friendships or coping with stressful situations. In many cultures, the role of machismo (as in Latin American cultures), the importance of male sexuality, is recognized as a key factor in shaping drinking patterns (e.g., 21). Thus excessive drinking celebrates male courage, sexual prowess, maturity, and the ability to take risks, including sexual risks. The association of masculinity and drinking and the use of alcohol as a means of coping with stress by men are key factors behind the rising toll of alcohol-related premature mortality in Eastern European men (22).

Third, alcohol consumption among men often takes the form of binge drinking, typically outside of the home, with other men (e.g., 23, 24). A study from Papua New Guinea, for example, reported that men tend to drink in groups, usually with a goal to get drunk (2). Drink-diary studies of male hazardous drinkers in India reported that binge drinking was significantly associated with the use of traditional and illicit alcohols (25). Beverage choice was related to socioeconomic status, with cost and ease of access being key determinants. In Mexico and some other Latin American countries, the legacy of fiesta has been identified as an important influence on male binge drinking (2).

The Relationship Between Alcohol Use and Mental Health

It must be acknowledged that the evidence base for the association of alcohol use and mental health in developing countries is weak, particularly from a population perspective. Alcohol dependence and harmful alcohol use are mental disorders in their own right in WHO's *International Statistical Classification of Diseases and Related Health Problems (ICD 10)* (26). For the purpose of this section, however, this paper will concentrate on their association with other mental disorders.

A number of important recent studies of high-risk populations in developing countries indicate moderate levels of comorbidity between alcohol abuse and mental illness. A study in São Paulo, Brazil, revealed that the prevalence of substance misuse among Brazilians with severe mental illness was lower than in developed countries (27). Nevertheless, the very presence of comorbidity worsens the prognosis and impact of mental disorders. Another Brazilian study reported an association between severity of alcohol dependence and psychiatric symptoms, stressing the importance of early detection (28). In a study from India, a linear relationship was found between comorbidity of mental disorders and alcohol and poorer quality of life (29).

Population-based studies reveal a strong association among hazardous drinking, poor mental health (especially, depressive and anxiety disorders), and suicide. For example, two studies on the association of alcohol use and mental health were carried out on a sample of male industrial workers in Goa, India (23, 24). A survey of 1013 workers found that one-fifth of all respondents were hazardous drinkers (24). In general, these men had begun drinking at an earlier age and had lower educational levels than nonhazardous drinkers. While hazardous drinkers often recognized that they had a drinking problem, only a small proportion (14%) had sought help. Hazardous drinkers were significantly more likely to suffer from a common mental disorder (depressive or anxiety disorders) or to have experienced an adverse health outcome, such as hospital admission. This study demonstrated a significant degree of comorbidity between common mental disorders and hazardous drinking, similar to that reported by researchers in developed countries (30, 31).

In a subsequent case-control investigation of the impact of alcohol consumption, two groups of drinkers (hazardous and nonhazardous or moderate drinkers) were compared with a group of abstinent men (23). Hazardous drinkers reported a higher number of sick leave days, increased rates of tobacco use, more frequent injury in the form of fractures, higher disability scores, more money spent on health, and poorer mental health than their moderate-drinking or abstinent counterparts. Whereas hazardous drinkers did not report financial difficulties, their spouses were more likely to attribute financial difficulties to their husbands' drinking. The study did not find any trends suggesting adverse impact of moderate drinking on any of these indicators. As compared with moderate drinkers, hazardous drinkers tended to drink alone, in bars, and preferred noncommercial alcoholic beverages, which are cheaper and have relatively high alcohol concentration. These findings suggest that the adverse association between male alcohol use and mental health in India is concentrated among men who drink hazardously.

Population-based studies reveal a strong association among hazardous drinking, poor mental health (especially, depressive and anxiety disorders), and suicide.

Similar relationships have been reported elsewhere in the world. In some Eastern European countries, a strong association between per capita alcohol consumption and suicide rates has been reported (1). In Chile, in the early 1980s, 38.6% of suicides were identified as "alcohol related"; a more recent study from Ethiopia revealed a linear relationship between adolescent suicide attempts and alcohol consumption (1). Several causal explanations have been cited. For example, alcohol may disinhibit suicidal impulses (and aggression in general), whereas chronic and heavy alcohol use may lead to a gradual disintegration of the person's social life, depression, and, thus, an elevated risk of suicide (1).

Another important consequence of alcohol consumption in developing countries is related to mental health of individuals living with problem drinkers. Several studies from developing countries have shown higher levels of family dysfunction and family violence among alcohol-dependent people and alcohol abusers (23). In studies conducted either with samples of alcohol-dependent subjects or in clinical situations, spouses (usually, female) of alcoholics were reported to suffer from significant stress levels and various physical and mental health problems. Studies of individuals in primary care in India showed significantly higher rates of depressive and anxiety disorders among women (32); concerns about spousal drinking behavior and the related experience of domestic violence were key risk factors. Higher rates of common mental disorders in women have been found in virtually all studies from developing countries (and, indeed, in developed countries); gender disadvantage, intimate partner violence, and alcoholism were cited as major factors to explain this increased risk (33). A recent community survey of women in India has confirmed these hypotheses; depressive and anxiety disorders were strongly—and independently—associated with intimate partner violence and concerns about spouses' drinking habits (34).

Implications

The evidence base on the prevalence of alcohol use and alcohol use disorders in developing countries presents a mixed picture. Although the overall use of alcohol at the population level is relatively low, with high abstention rates, drinking patterns among those who do drink are often hazardous. Poor people are more likely to consume cheaper, traditional alcohols, linked to some adverse health and social consequences. The consumption of alcohol is heavily gendered and is characterized by a high proportion of hazardous drinking among men. Hazardous drinkers do not only consume large amounts of alcohol, but also do so in high-risk patterns, such as drinking alone and bingeing. Hazardous drinking is strongly associated with common mental disorders and suicide and domestic violence, especially among women. Rates of alcohol dependence are relatively low in many developing countries, but this condition is associated with high levels of disability and mortality. The recent report "Global Burden of Disease and Risk Factors" (5) has highlighted the contribution of alcohol, as a risk factor, to the global burden of disease; alcohol use disorders account for nearly 4% of the attributable-disease burden. The disease outcomes assessed include depression and suicide. This burden was concentrated in men under the age of 60 years.

Although the overall use of alcohol [in developing countries] . . . is relatively low, . . . drinking patterns among those who do drink are often hazardous.

On the other hand, there is little evidence on the harms—or benefits—of moderate drinking. Moderate consumption may be beneficial to individuals, although the "less tangible benefits of conviviality, sociability, and in some cases social solidarity are difficult to quantify" (1, p. 46). Little attention has been paid to these nonquantifiable aspects of moderate consumption as they relate to mental health and the general quality of life. Important research questions remain on health and social impacts of different patterns of alcohol consumption in developing countries. Such research should not only focus on the negative impact of hazardous drinking, but also address the potential benefits of moderate consumption. The use of qualitative research methods would be highly relevant in such inquiries.

The major challenge in terms of alcohol use and mental health in developing countries is to reduce the rates of hazardous drinking and alcohol dependence in the population. This may be achieved, for example, by linking alcohol taxation to the level of alcohol content in a given beverage and by strengthening the enforcement of licensing to sell drinks with high alcohol concentration. In addition, since relatively few hazardous drinkers seek help because of stigma, lack of services, and lack of awareness, a concerted campaign is needed to educate the community about the health dimensions of hazardous drinking and definitions of moderate consumption, combined with community-based interventions. This strategy provides the potential for primary prevention.

References

1. World Health Organization. Global Status Report on Alcohol. Geneva: WHO; 1999.

2. Riley L, Marshall M. Alcohol and Public Health in 8 Developing Countries. Geneva: World Health Organization; 1999.

3. World Health Organization. The World Health Report 2001: Mental health: New Understanding, New Hope. Geneva: WHO; 2001.

4. Lopez A, Mathers C, Ezzati M, Jamison D, Murray C. Global Burden of Disease and Risk Factors. Washington (DC): Oxford University Press and the World Bank; 2006.

5. Kessler R, Bergland P, Demler O, Jin R, Walters EE. Lifetime prevalence and age-of-onset distributions of DSM-IV disorders in the National Comorbidity Survey Replication. Arch Gen Psychiatry. 2005;62: 593–602.

6. World Health Organization. Mental Health Atlas. Geneva: WHO; 2005.

7. Linden M, Lecrubier Y, Bellantuono C, Benkert O, Kisely S, Simon G. The prescribing of psychotropic drugs by primary care physicians: An international collaborative study. J Clin Psychopharmacol. 1999;19:132–140.

8. Jamison KR. The many stigmas of mental illness. Lancet. 2006;367:533–534.

9. National Human Rights Commission. Quality Assurance in Mental Health. New Delhi: NHRC; 1999.

10. Sachs JD, McArthur JW. The Millennium Project: A plan for meeting the Millennium Development Goals. Lancet. 2005;365:347–353.

11. World Health Organization. WHO and the Millennium Development Goals. Available at: http://www.who.int/mdg/en/. Accessed March 24, 2005.

12. Miranda JJ, Patel V. Achieving the Millennium Development Goals: Does mental health play a role? PLoS Med. 2005;2:e291.

13. Patel V, Prince M. Maternal psychological morbidity and low birth weight in India. Br J Psychiatry. 2006;188:284–285.

14. Patel V, Rahman M, Jacob K, Hughes M. Effect of maternal mental health on infant growth in low income countries: New evidence from South Asia. BMJ. 2004;328:820–823.

15. Collins PY, Holman AR, Freeman MC, Patel V. What is the relevance of mental health to HIV/AIDS care and treatment programs in developing countries? A systematic review. AIDS. 2006;20:1571–1582.

16. Patel V, Kleinman A. Poverty and common mental disorders in developing countries. Bull World Health Organ. 2003;81:609–615.

17. Chatterjee S, Patel V, Chatterjee A, Weiss H. Evaluation of a community based rehabilitation model for chronic schizophrenia in a rural region of India. Br J Psychiatry. 2003;182:57–62.

18. Patel V, Araya R, Bolton P. Treating depression in the developing world. Trop Med Int Health. 2004;9:539–541.

19. Wu Z, Detels R, Zhang J, Li V, Li J. Community-based trial to prevent drug use among youths in Yunnan, China. Am J Public Health. 2002;92:1952–1957.

20. Patel V, Thara R. Meeting the Mental Health Needs of Developing Countries: NGO Innovations in India. New Delhi: Sage; 2003.

21. Pyne HH, Claeson M, Correia M. Gender dimensions of alcohol consumption and alcohol-related problems in Latin America and the Caribbean: World Bank Discussion Paper No. 433. Washington (DC): The World Bank; 2002.

22. Bromet EJ, Gluzman SF, Paniotto VI, Webb CP, Tintle NL, Zakhozha V, et al. Epidemiology of psychiatric and alcohol disorders in Ukraine: Findings from the Ukraine World Mental Health survey. Soc Psychiatry Psychiatr Epidemiol. 2005;40:681–690.

23. Gaunekar G, Patel V, Rane A. The impact and patterns of hazardous drinking amongst male industrial workers in Goa, India. Soc Psychiatry Psychiatr Epidemiol. 2005;40:267–275.

24. Chagas Silva M, Gaunekar G, Patel V, Kukalekar DS, Fernandes J. The prevalence and correlates of hazardous drinking in industrial workers: A study from Goa, India. Alcohol Alcohol. 2003;38:79–83.

25. Gaunekar G, Patel V, Jacob KS, Vankar G, Mohan D, Rane A, et al. Drinking patterns of hazardous drinkers: A multicenter study in India. In: Haworth A, Simpson R, eds. Moonshine Markets: Issues in Unrecorded Alcohol Beverage Production and Consumption. New York: Brunner-Routledge; 2004:125–144.

26. World Health Organization. International Statistical Classification of Diseases and Related Health Problems, 10th Revision. 2nd ed. Geneva: World Health Organization; 2005.

27. Rossi Menezes P, Ratto LC. Prevalence of substance misuse among individuals with severe mental illness in Sao Paulo. Soc Psychiatry Psychiatr Epidemiol. 2004;39:212–217.

28. Lima AF, Pechansky F, Fleck MP, De Boni R. Association between psychiatric symptoms and severity of alcohol dependence in a sample of Brazilian men. J Nerv Ment Dis. 2005;193:126–130.

29. Singh J, Mattoo SK, Sharan P, Basu D. Quality of life and its correlates in patients with dual diagnosis of bipolar affective disorder and substance dependence. Bipolar Disord. 2005;7:187–191.

30. Hickie IB, Koschera A, Davenport TA, Naismith SL, Scott EM. Comorbidity of common mental disorders and alcohol or other substance misuse in Australian general practice. Med J Aust. 2001;175(Suppl):S31–36.

31. Lynskey MT. The comorbidity of alcohol dependence and affective disorders: Treatment implications. Drug Alcohol Depend. 1998;52:201–209.

32. Patel V, Pereira J, Coutinho L, Fernandes R, Fernandes J, Mann A. Poverty, psychological disorder and disability in primary care attenders in Goa, India. Br J Psychiatry. 1998;172:533–536.

33. Patel V, Araya R, de Lima M, Ludermir A, Todd C. Women, poverty and common mental disorders in four restructuring societies. Soc Sci Med. 1999;49:1461–1471.

34. Patel V, Kirkwood BR, Pednekar S, Pereira B, Barros P, Fernandes J, et al. Gender disadvantage and reproductive health risk factors for common mental disorder in women: A community survey in India. Arch Gen Psychiatry. 2006;63:404–413.

35. World Health Organization. Global status report on alcohol 2004. Geneva: World Health Organization.

VIEWPOINT

In Ireland, Alcohol Abuse Is Related to Mental Illness and Suicide Among Young People

Alcohol Action Ireland

Alcohol Action Ireland is a national Irish charity devoted to alcohol-related issues. In the following viewpoint, the organization says that suicide is a leading cause of death among young Irish adults. Alcohol Action Ireland also asserts that there is a strong link between alcohol use and suicide. The Irish drinking rate, according to the organization, is very high by European standards, and the rate of binge drinking among young Irish people is also high. Alcohol Action Ireland concludes that the high rate of suicide in Ireland is related to the high rate of drinking. It recommends programs to reduce alcohol consumption in Ireland.

As you read, consider the following questions:

1. Why does Alcohol Action Ireland say that drinking among teenagers is particularly worrying?
2. According to the World Health Organization, by how much does the abuse of alcohol increase the risk of suicide?

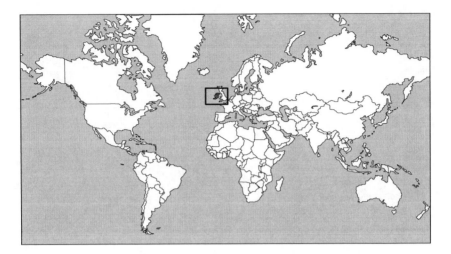

3. What does Alcohol Action Ireland say its overall objectives are in terms of reducing alcohol-related suicide?

Suicide is the leading cause of death in young Irish adults. Since 1998, more people have died as a result of suicide than in road traffic accidents, deaths from suicide exceeding those from road traffic accidents by as many as 100 people each year. Up to 500 suicide deaths are reported each year.

Drinking in Ireland

Alcohol can contribute to worsening an individual's problems if they already have a preexisting mental health issue, while ongoing problem alcohol use can lead to an individual developing mental health issues. Alcohol can affect our ability to cope, manage and overcome everyday stresses and significant life events such as unemployment or bereavement. It can also reduce inhibitions enough for an individual to act on suicidal thoughts which they might never have done if not under the influence of alcohol.

Despite the contributory role alcohol plays in worsening or developing mental health problems, little research has been done in Ireland to explore the reasons why we drink and how this might link with rates of mental health problems such as anxiety, depression, self-harm and potentially suicide.

Ireland is among the heaviest drinking nations in Europe, exceeding the European average by more than 20%. According to the most recent Europe-wide survey, Irish children aged 15 and 16 have "a major issue about drunkenness". More girls (44%) than boys (42%) said they had been 'binge drinking' at least once in the previous month.

Ireland is among the heaviest drinking nations in Europe, exceeding the European average by more than 20%.

Teenagers are effectively imitating what they see the adults in the wider Irish society doing, which is drinking to excessive levels. What is surprising is the apparent shock expressed at the fact that Irish teenagers are emulating Irish adults when it comes to alcohol use. Biological and emotional developmental issues make drinking among teenagers particularly worrying:

- Biologically teenagers' brains are still developing and alcohol affects, in particular, the areas of the brain responsible for memory and impulse control

- Adolescence can be a challenging time as young people navigate new experiences and stresses for the first time: Alcohol is being added to situations where there is no preexisting "road map" and may render the individual particularly vulnerable to exploitation or danger

- Behaviour patterns that can last a lifetime are being established during this formative period. Adult heavy drinkers generally established their drinking patterns in their teens

High Suicide Rates

Considering Ireland has the fifth highest rate of suicide among 15- to 24-year-olds in the 26 countries of the EU [European Union] the following questions have yet to be adequately answered:

- Is enough being done to facilitate young people to develop good mental health?

- Is enough being done to help those who have mental health problems to manage and/or recover from their conditions in terms of appropriateness of services and equality of access?

- What is the status of the mental health resources pledged under Towards 2016 [a social partnership agreement developed by the Irish government] such as community mental health teams?

- Is enough being done to challenge the contributory factors of 500 young people taking their own lives every year?

Although many factors are involved in suicide, patterns of problem alcohol use contribute significantly to the high rate of suicide among young Irish men in particular.

The connection between alcohol use and suicide has been highlighted in numerous reports, both Irish and international. One Irish study of people from three counties who died as a result of suicide, found that more than half had alcohol in their blood; those aged less than 30 were more likely to have had alcohol in their blood at the time of death.

The World Health Organization has estimated that the risk of suicide when a person is currently abusing alcohol is eight times greater than if they were not abusing alcohol. Closer to home, a report from the UK [United Kingdom] Mental Health Foundation states that as many as 65% of suicides were related to excessive drinking and identifies alcohol problems as one of the highest risk factors for suicide. That report identifies a strong link between alcohol use and thoughts of suicide, suicide attempts and completed suicides among young people under the age of 24. Alcohol use can act as a factor in suicide in a number of ways:

- A recent HSE [Health and Safety Executive] report tells us that "*alcohol can facilitate suicide by increasing impulsivity, changing mood and deepening depression*"

- Self-harm or suicide can take place after just one drinking session. A person doesn't have to be a heavy drinker or even a regular drinker: Just one occasion of heavy drinking can reduce inhibitions enough to self-harm or act on suicidal thoughts

- Alcohol initially produces feelings of happiness and well-being but can lead to a significant lowering in mood hours after use or in the following days, an experience which is sometimes accompanied by feelings of hopelessness. If someone is already experiencing a degree of depression, the fall in mood can lead to suicidal ideas

- Ongoing abuse of alcohol is itself a major contributory factor in depression and suicidal behaviour

- In 2006/2007 alcohol was a factor in 41% of all cases of deliberate self-harm. It was more common in cases involving men (44%) than women (38%)

The connection between alcohol use and suicide has been highlighted in numerous reports, both Irish and international.

In the UK, a country with similar drinking patterns to Ireland, a recent study found that many people drink alcohol to help them cope with emotions or situations they would otherwise find difficult to manage. In other words, they drink to change mood or mental state. Alcohol is also used to self-medicate, to relieve the symptoms of anxiety and depression. The same report also found that stressed mood leads to increased alcohol consumption, which explains why another study found that "relaxation" was the key reason cited for people drinking.

Tolerance of alcohol increases with use, so that an individual needs increasing amounts of alcohol to decrease their anxiety or to medicate their depression. Secondly, when self-medicating with alcohol, it is difficult to know how much is enough. Following the initial feeling of well-being from the first drink, alcohol acts as a depressant, and feelings of anxiety and depression can quickly resurface. Indeed, alcohol use can exaggerate underlying feelings, which is why some people become angry, tearful, or aggressive after a few drinks.

A Way Forward

Alcohol Action Ireland fully supports the objective and recommendations of Reach Out, the national suicide prevention plan as it relates to suicide and alcohol use. The overall objectives are to:

- Challenge permissive, harmful attitudes to alcohol abuse

- Help to reduce overall consumption rates and

- Raise awareness of the link between alcohol and/or substance abuse and suicidal behaviour

The actions which aim to achieve this objective are to:

- Implement the recommendations of the two reports of the Strategic Task Force on Alcohol. The recommendations are to:
  - regulate availability
  - control promotion of alcohol

- enhance society's capacity to respond to alcohol-related harm
- prevent and reduce alcohol-related harm in public, private and working environments
- involve the alcohol beverage industry in reducing harms caused by alcohol
- provide information and education; put in place effective treatment services
- support nongovernment organizations
- research and monitor progress
- reduce drink-driving

- Review the current provision of alcohol and addiction treatment services making recommendations for future service development, especially for people experiencing both mental health and alcohol/addiction problems together

If we are seriously interested in tackling the main cause of death of young Irish adults, we need to reduce the overall level of alcohol consumption and make the change to reduced and healthier patterns of drinking in Ireland.

The Smoking Ban in the United Kingdom Raises Difficult Issues for Mental Health Care Professionals and Patients

Deborah Cornah

Deborah Cornah is a researcher in the Department of Psychology at the University of Southampton. In the following viewpoint, she says that patients with mental health problems smoke more frequently and have more trouble quitting than people in the general population. She reports that Britain is establishing a smoking ban that will effectively ban smoking in mental health treatment facilities. She says that staff and patients are both concerned about the effects. She argues that mental health providers need to offer their patients more help with smoking cessation strategies, especially since many patients would like to quit but have difficulty on their own.

As you read, consider the following questions:

1. What role does Cornah say that dopamine can play in both nicotine use and depression?
2. According to Cornah, why have some argued that cognitive behavioral therapy is effective at helping people with depression give up smoking?

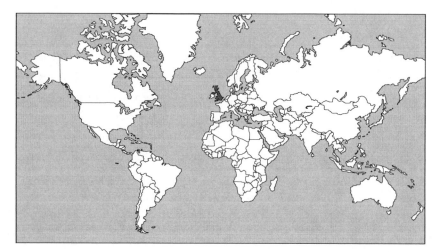

3. What are three specific concluding recommendations Cornah makes to help mental health patients and professionals adapt to the new smoking ban?

A smoking ban covering all public places and workplaces comes into effect in England on 1 July 2007. It has been the subject of fierce debate. Up to 15% of smokers have said they would quit in response to a smoking ban, and the government predicts an estimated 600,000 people will give up smoking as a result of the change in the law.

The Smoking Ban and Mental Health

The smoking ban is likely to bring many welcome health benefits for the whole population, but there are a number of concerns about the likely effects of the ban on people with mental health problems. Firstly, the ban will leave anyone whose temporary home is also a public place and/or workplace, unable to smoke in their own home. This applies to people living for long periods in mental health inpatient units. The government has weighed the rights of smokers in mental health units against the rights of nonsmokers and staff to breathe smoke-free air and have concluded that the ban should apply in mental health units.

The ban highlights a range of issues covering many more people living in the community, from those with common mental health problems such as anxiety and depression to people with severe and enduring mental health problems such as schizophrenia. Giving up smoking is widely acknowledged to be very difficult for the general population, but comparatively little consideration is given to the extra needs of people with mental health problems. Mounting evidence shows that people with mental health problems are more likely to smoke and less likely to be successful at quitting than the general population. Their needs can and should be addressed to help them to abide by the smoking ban as easily and positively as possible, and also to improve their chances of being among the 600,000 who are likely to quit successfully following the ban.

Because prisons, care homes and hospices are considered 'private dwellings' they do not have to conform to the smoke-free legislation. In some countries, mental health units are also exempt. English legislation, however, will offer only a limited exemption to the smoking ban in residential mental health units, allowing smoking in bedrooms or rooms used only for smoking until the 1st July 2008, after which date all enclosed parts of the unit will be required to comply with the ban.

Mounting evidence shows that people with mental health problems are more likely to smoke and less likely to be successful at quitting than the general population.

This decision has divided opinion among mental health service users, staff, policy makers and practitioners. Concerns have been expressed by many people about how a ban will work in mental health units. Major worries include the distress caused by stopping people from smoking when they are in a mental health crisis. Much research from other countries draws the conclusion that implementation of smoke-free policies in residential mental health units has not resulted in many of the negative outcomes anticipated in those countries, but concern remains high. Research has also highlighted the often inadequate availability or suitability of smoking cessation strategies and support in mental health units. This points to the need for services to develop useful and effective cessation strategies, where nicotine dependence is taken into account as a routine part of care planning, and help with quitting is routinely offered.

Links Between Mental Health and Smoking

Although adult tobacco use has shown a slight decline in the last decade among the general population, smoking among people with mental health problems has shown no appreciable reduction.

Current estimates show that approximately 26% of the adult population (or 13 million people) smoke. An estimated 40% of people with mental health problems smoke. Of the 26% of the general adult population who smoke, the proportion smoking more than 20 cigarettes a day ('heavy smokers') has fallen, from 55% to 33% for males and 40% to 27% for females. In contrast, the figures for people with mental health problems remain stable, and high. Studies of psychiatric patients in mental health units show that up to 70% smoke and around 50% are heavy smokers. People with mental health problems living in the community smoke less, but still more than people in the general population, with up to 40% smoking and 30% smoking heavily.

The risk factors associated with smoking—social deprivation, stress, alcohol use and poverty, among others—are also associated with poorer mental health and therefore it is unsurprising that people with mental health problems smoke more. However, research has shown that smoking is more common among people with mental health problems, even when these other factors have been taken into account.

It is also important to point out that among people with undiagnosed or subclinical mental health problems, smoking is believed to be an important way of coping with stress, anxiety or low mood. Studies have shown that people who smoke report more feelings of stress. An increased number of people trying to give up smoking following the ban will need to look for alternative ways of coping with stress and anxiety such as exercise and social activities. They are likely to come into contact with providers of smoking cessation services and information should be available to meet their needs.

Current estimates show that approximately 26% of the adult population . . . smoke. An estimated 40% of people with mental health problems smoke.

The biological factors involved in smoking relate to the physiology of the brain and its response to nicotine. Nicotine is biphasic, meaning that it first has a stimulating and then a depressing effect in the brain. When a person smokes, a dose of nicotine reaches the brain within about ten seconds of inhalation, producing a positive feeling. Initially, nicotine can produce effects such as improved mood and concentration, decreased anger and stress, relaxed muscles, increased heart rate and reduced appetite. However, this also leads to alterations in the neurotransmitter systems in the brain (especially dopamine pathways), which then leads to nicotine withdrawal symptoms, including headaches, irritability, difficulty in concentration, increased appetite and drowsiness. Then smoking can become cyclical because it temporarily reduces these withdrawal symptoms.

In the UK [United Kingdom], one study put smoking among people with depression at around 56%, compared with 26% of the general population. People with depression report more severe withdrawal symptoms during attempts to give up smoking, and are at increased risk of developing a new episode of depression for up to six months after quitting. This may be due in part to the role that certain neurotransmitters such as dopamine play in both smoking and depression. Nicotine has been shown to stimulate dopamine release in the brain for a short time, and dopamine is often found to be depleted or inadequate in people with depression. The artificial supply of dopamine from smoking cigarettes eventually depletes the brain of its own resources, and depression may worsen due to the diminishing supply.

People with schizophrenia are more likely to smoke, and smoke more heavily than other populations. Rates of smoking among people with schizophrenia remain stable at about 70–74%, regardless of whether they are living in mental health units or within the community. Many studies have explored the reasons why people with schizophrenia are more likely to smoke and suggestions have included the possibility that they find it harder to quit once they start and that they start smoking younger. There are also explanations that consider other associated risk factors involved in both smoking and schizophrenia, like substance or alcohol abuse and nutritional deficiencies. In addition, some studies argue that smoking is associated with the culture of inpatient psychiatric wards.

One of the most popular explanations proposed to account for the increased smoking rates among people with schizophrenia is 'self-medication'. That is, people with schizophrenia use smoking—and the dose of nicotine it provides them with—to control or manage some of the symptoms associated with their illness and to reduce some of the side effects of their medication. There is some evidence to support this biological explanation of smoking and it centres around the role dopamine plays in mood and motivation. However, a

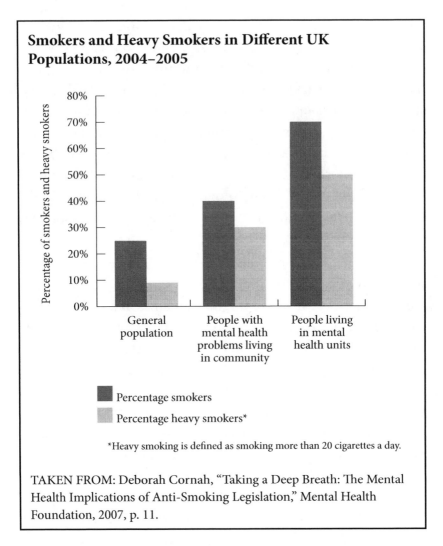

Smokers and Heavy Smokers in Different UK Populations, 2004–2005

Percentage of smokers and heavy smokers

- Percentage smokers
- Percentage heavy smokers*

*Heavy smoking is defined as smoking more than 20 cigarettes a day.

TAKEN FROM: Deborah Cornah, "Taking a Deep Breath: The Mental Health Implications of Anti-Smoking Legislation," Mental Health Foundation, 2007, p. 11.

recent Cochrane review [reviews that systematically look at all the health care research on given topics] found no studies that support the theory that nicotine alleviates the symptoms of schizophrenia.

What is clear is that many smokers with mental health problems say that they would like to stop smoking, but struggle when they try to do so. They need effective support to help them stop smoking.

Smoking Cessation and Mental Health

Cessation rates among smokers with mental health problems are two to three times lower than in the general population. This, for reasons outlined above, points to the possibility that mainstream smoking cessation programmes are not adequately addressing the needs of people with mental health problems. A number of methods [can be considered], . . . including talking and drug-based approaches, as well as approaches that combine the two, for example nicotine replacement therapy [in which the patient receives nicotine by a means other than smoking, such as a nicotine patch] combined with cognitive behavioural therapy (CBT) [in which smokers are given counseling and therapy].

Cessation rates among smokers with mental health problems are two to three times lower than in the general population.

Some have argued that CBT is effective at helping people with depression give up smoking because it helps them challenge negative attitudes that stop them from quitting and helps them adopt alternative ways of coping with difficult feelings such as stress and anxiety that may lead them to turn to cigarettes. It has been argued that improvements can be made in quit rates for heavy smokers with depression or with people whose depression is recurrent if the standard smoking cessation CBT includes a component directly concerned with the smoker's depression. Combined approaches have been found to work in studies of people with depression and also schizophrenia.

The report also examines good practice in mental health services which may help with the implementation of the smoking ban. . . . Given the high rates of smoking among people with mental health problems there is still a comparative lack of evidence about which methods are most effective for them.

If quit rates among people with mental health problems are to increase, both in inpatient services where smoking will be banned and within the community, we need to understand which cessation strategies recognise the different and related reasons for smoking among these groups and use them. These groups should be offered a combination of drug-based and talking therapies.

Recommendations for Better Overall Care

In light of the evidence ... , the following recommendations are made:

1. Primary care staff should be made aware of higher smoking rates and more reported difficulties in quitting among people with mental health problems and of any specialist help available, so they can refer effectively

2. People providing information on smoking cessation including help lines should be made aware of the needs of people with mental health problems, and should be able to signpost them to other help and support

3. Commissioners need to ensure that smoking cessation services including group therapies are tailored to meet the needs of vulnerable groups including mental health service users

4. Staff in mental health services must offer nicotine replacement therapy and other smoking cessation support

5. Mental health services need to commission specialist help with smoking cessation such as CBT

6. Patients in both inpatient and community services must be offered help with smoking cessation as part of their care package

7. Staff in mental health services should understand nicotine withdrawal symptoms and how they can exacerbate mental distress, so that they can respond effectively

8. Information should be made widely available to staff, service users and visitors to mental health services about how their environment will change as a result of the smoking ban, and of any help that is available with smoking cessation

9. Inpatient units need to ensure that there is a sheltered outdoor space that smokers can access, and where necessary, regular escorted visits to these spaces should be offered as a priority

10. Any aggression or violence toward patients and staff in inpatient settings that are believed to be linked to the smoking ban should be monitored and reported to senior managers in MHTs [mental health trusts]

To Address Substance Abuse and Mental Illness, Southeast Asia Needs to Shift to Community-Based Health Care

Vijay Chandra

Vijay Chandra is regional advisor to the World Health Organization's regional office for Southeast Asia. In the following viewpoint, he says that mental health services in Southeast Asia are concentrated in hospitals and argues that a switch to community-based care is necessary. He also points out that Southeast Asia has a number of serious substance abuse issues that should be handled through community-based care. He says that stigma against mental illness needs to be overcome in the region and that programs must be culturally appropriate and accessible to the population.

As you read, consider the following questions:

1. In what ways does Chandra say that the region is particularly affected by the problems of substance abuse?

2. What are the five A's that Chandra says are essential to provide community-based care?

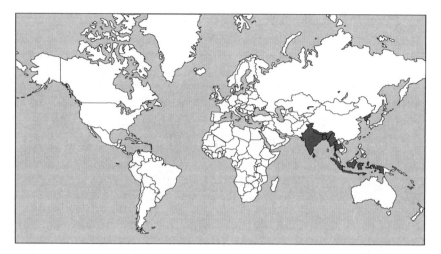

3. At the community level, who does Chandra say should manage most psychiatric conditions, and what makes this necessary?

[The mission of the World Health Organization's regional office for Southeast Asia is] to support member countries in Southeast Asia in the promotion of mental health and the reduction of the burden associated with mental and neurological disorders, including substance abuse and harm from alcohol, through mental health promotion and delivery of appropriate care at all levels of society. This will also include the collection of information on determinants of mental health within populations for appropriate planning and effective interventions.

Community-Based Care and Substance Abuse

In the member countries of the region, mental health activities have generally concentrated on hospital-based psychiatry and neurology. However, there is increasing awareness of the need to shift the emphasis to community-based mental health programmes. This is the renewed focus of the unit. The unit addresses mental health issues, neurosciences and substance abuse.

The region is particularly affected by the problem of substance abuse. A part of the notorious [opium-producing] "Golden Triangle" (Myanmar [also known as Burma], Laos, and Thailand) falls within the region. India has become a major trans-shipment point for hard drugs from Pakistan. The ill effects of excessive consumption of alcohol have become a major public health problem in the region.

There is an urgent need to sensitize governments on the importance of mental health and to clearly define the goals and objectives of a community-based mental health programme. Mental health services should be integrated into the overall primary health care system along with innovative community-based programmes. There is also an urgent need to sensitize governments on the importance of substance dependence, including the ill effects of alcohol, and to clearly define the goals and objectives to control substance dependence.

There is an urgent need to sensitize governments on the importance of mental health and to clearly define the goals and objectives of a community-based mental health programme.

The Five A's

In SEAR [Southeast Asia region] member countries, mental health programmes have generally concentrated on hospital-based psychiatry. However, there is increasing awareness in these countries of the need to shift the emphasis to community-based mental health programmes. The WHO [World Health Organization] regional office for Southeast Asia is concentrating on supporting member countries on the development of community-based mental health programmes and also programmes for prevention of harm from alcohol and substances of abuse. The programmes will be culturally and gender appropriate and reach out to all segments of the population, including marginalized groups.

There are many barriers to the implementation of community mental health projects and programmes. While some countries have developed mental health policies, there has not been adequate implementation. Governments urgently need to be sensitized on the importance of mental health and to clearly define the goals and objectives for community-based mental health programmes. Mental health services should be integrated into the overall primary health care system. At the same time, innovative community-based programmes need to be developed and research into relevant issues and traditional practices promoted. Communities have to be educated and informed about mental and neurological illnesses to remove the numerous myths and misconceptions about these conditions. But most important, the stigma and the discrimination associated with mental illness must be removed.

The regional office is developing strategies for community-based programmes based on five A's: availability, acceptability, accessibility, affordable medications and assessment.

- *Availability*: Services which will address at least the minimum needs of populations in mental and neurological disorders should be available to everyone regardless of where they live. The key questions are: what are the minimum services needed and who will deliver them?

- *Acceptability*: Large segments of populations in the countries continue to perpetuate superstitions and false beliefs about mental and neurological illnesses. Many believe that these illnesses are due to "evil spirits". Thus, even if appropriate medical services are made available, they would rather go to sorcerers and faith healers. Populations need to be informed and educated about the nature of neuropsychiatric illnesses.

- *Accessibility*: Services should be available to the community, in the community, and at convenient times. If a worker has to give up his daily wages, and travel a substantial distance to see a medical professional who is only available for a few hours a day, he/she is unlikely to seek these services.

- *Affordable medications*: Frequently, medications are beyond the reach of the poor. Every effort should be made to provide essential medications uninterruptedly and at a reasonable cost. Thus, government policies in terms of pricing and the role of the pharmaceutical industry in distribution and pricing become critical.

- *Assessment*: Being new, these programmes need to be continuously assessed to ensure appropriateness and cost-effectiveness. Changes in the ongoing programmes based on impartial evaluations are essential.

Services which will address at least the minimum needs of populations in mental neurological disorders should be available to everyone regardless of where they live.

Mental Health Strategies for Southeast Asia

Community mental health:

1. Development/implementation of mental health policy
2. Compiling information on mental disorders and mental health systems

3. Innovative community-based management programmes for mental and neurological conditions causing high morbidity in the community

4. Enhancing awareness campaigns

5. Support for research on indigenous practices and medications

6. Promotion of mental well-being in the community

Control of substance dependence:

1. Facilitation of collaboration between member countries and SEARO [Southeast Asia regional office] and HQ [headquarters]

2. Compiling information on burden from substance dependence

3. Enhancing advocacy and awareness campaigns

4. Innovative community-based management programmes

5. Support for research on unique local issues related to substance dependence

Prevention of harm from alcohol use:

1. Empower individuals and communities to prevent harm from alcohol use and abuse

2. Achieve a sustained reduction in per capita consumption of alcohol, based on national multi-sectoral approaches and mobilization of civil society

Disaster mental health:

The tsunami disaster of December 2004 had a devastating impact on select member countries of Southeast Asia region. Programmes for the mental health and psychosocial relief efforts to affected countries were developed and implemented. Similar strategies were also successfully implemented in the . . . super cyclone [Sidr] in Bangladesh [in 2007] and . . . super cyclone [Nargis] in Myanmar [in 2008].

Strengthening the primary health care system to deliver essential mental health care:

There is a scarcity of mental health professionals in the Southeast Asia region. Most psychiatric conditions are manageable at the community level by general practitioners (GPs). [We are providing] training audiovisual material . . . designed to enable GPs to diagnose and treat such patients in the community. Using a combination of graphics and visuals, the film lucidly explains the signs, symptoms and management of common mental health conditions which GPs are most likely to encounter during their practice.

Eastern Europe Has Unique Problems with Mental Illness and Substance Abuse

Jane Salvage and Rob Keukens

Jane Salvage is a visiting professor at the Florence Nightingale School of Nursing and Midwifery, King's College London, and the author of The Politics of Nursing; *Rob Keukens is a lecturer at HAN University of Applied Sciences in the Netherlands. In the following viewpoint, they argue that the transition from communism to capitalism in Eastern Europe has created serious mental health and substance abuse problems as people and governments struggle to adjust to major change. They say that HIV/ AIDS infection is also a serious issue that has been exacerbated and that this development increases mental illness and drug abuse problems. They say more training for medical personnel, more services, and greater community awareness are vital to address these problems.*

As you read, consider the following questions:

1. According to the authors, how do some people who suffer from mental illness and poverty support themselves in Eastern Europe, and where do many of them end up?

Jane Salvage and Rob Keukens, "Tears of a Komsomol Girl: Perspectives on Dual Diagnosis from Eastern Europe," *Advances in Dual Diagnosis*, vol. 3, no. 3, August 2010, pp. 4–9. Copyright © 2010 by Emerald Group Publishing Limited. All rights reserved. Reproduced by permission.

2. Why do the authors suggest that drug use has risen in Eastern Europe after the fall of communism?

3. What are some of the bright spots in treatment of dual diagnosis, according to the authors?

The origins of this [viewpoint] lie in a chance meeting of two nurses in the Ministry of Health in Bucharest [the capital of Romania] around 1993. One of the authors, from England, was working as the regional nursing adviser for Europe for the World Health Organization (WHO); the other, from Holland, was visiting Romania as part of a mental health nursing reform project. Our meeting proved to be the beginning of a long-term personal friendship and professional collaboration. We have wide experience, mainly through WHO and the Global Initiative on Psychiatry, of working with mental health reformers in many different countries.

Here we explore the social context, prevalence and treatment of problems related to dual diagnosis in the region that is commonly—if inaccurately—known as Eastern Europe. We describe the historical and societal background and set out basic epidemiological information. We review what services are available for people with dual and triple diagnosis.[1] Finally, we outline the barriers to progress and make recommendations for improvements. We draw on an extensive literature search, as well as what we see in asylums, treatment centres, city centres and remote villages, and what we hear from service users, families, community leaders, health workers and policy makers. . . .

The term 'Eastern Europe' usually refers to the former eastern bloc of countries that lay within the Soviet Union and its sphere of influence. Just as it is impossible to give a single picture of dual diagnosis in Western Europe, a truly balanced picture of Eastern European developments would only be pos-

---

1. Dual diagnosis means a person has both mental illness and a substance abuse problem. Triple diagnosis is a dual diagnosis with HIV/AIDS.

sible through discussion of each country. Here, however, we can only sketch the overall situation—but it remains possible to make some meaningful generalisations, despite these countries' growing diversity. There is still remarkable homogeneity owing to the durability of their Communist legacy, and mental health care is one of many areas that has changed relatively little—shamefully little—since the collapse of the Soviet Union in 1989.

The Historical and Social Context

The 23 countries of Eastern Europe comprise a region with a common political history rather than any geographical or cultural coherence. The 15 republics of the Soviet Union gained full independence following its demise, Czechoslovakia and the former Yugoslavia split into different countries, and Germany was reunified. With more than 350 million people, the region stretches from central Europe to the far eastern Russian shores, and from the Arctic north to the Caucasus and central Asia.

Eastern Europe exemplifies the strong relationship between poverty and social deprivation, often accompanied by alcohol misuse and poor mental health.

The collapse of the Soviet Union brought many countries to the brink of chaos and dragged social and health structures down with it. Civil war, internal conflict, massive poverty, unemployment and migration were just some of the consequences of system breakdown and the forced march towards capitalism. For over 20 years, all these countries have been dealing with the impact of overwhelming internal and external pressures for transition to more liberal ideologies, market-oriented economics and civil society. The economic and social consequences were of varying profile and intensity, but even the most prosperous countries such as Hungary and Poland are now struggling to deal with the burdens arising from the global financial crisis.

These momentous upheavals continue to have a huge impact on health and psychosocial well-being. Rapid economic and social changes have been accompanied by a decline in mental and physical health and a sharp increase in substance abuse, prostitution, HIV and other sexually transmitted infections. Life expectancy has fallen, and the incidence of diseases previously controlled through primary health care and immunisation has risen. Rapidly declining socioeconomic conditions and increasing inequity have brought *'a sense of despair and hopelessness that is fertile ground for HIV transmission through increased risk behaviour including prostitution and drug use. A struggling economy means fewer resources for prevention and care'* [according to a 2003 paper by F. Hamers and A. Downs].

Eastern Europe exemplifies the strong relationship between poverty and social deprivation, often accompanied by alcohol misuse and poor mental health. Lack of work and income usually lowers self-esteem, leading to a greater risk of physical illness, depression and anxiety disorders, substance misuse and suicide. Nine of the 15 countries with the worst suicide rates worldwide are in Eastern Europe. Some people who suffer the double stigma of mental illness and poverty support themselves and their dependants through crime or sex work, and in the search for temporary relief from their symptoms they may damage their health through unprotected sex and abuse of alcohol and drugs. Many end up in prison, where they are exposed to yet more health risks and their hopes of future employment vanish.

Self-esteem, social cohesion and a sense of identity—some of the important factors that help protect people against mental illness and substance abuse—have been undermined, as reflected in high levels of violence, divorce and suicide. Social safety nets for the poor and the ill were full of holes or have disintegrated. Many of the most economically active and skilled young workers migrated, reducing family income. Meanwhile social and health problems not only exacerbated the problems of dual diagnosis, but also undermined the means of tackling them.

Elements of Dual Diagnosis in the Region

A large and growing number of people suffer temporarily or long-term from both a psychiatric condition and problems with substance use. . . . All the determinants of dual diagnosis are gaining a stronger hold in many other parts of Eastern Europe. Here we look briefly at each in turn and consider their lethal relationship with the alarming and rapid spread of HIV infection.

Alcohol consumption has reached alarming levels in Eastern Europe. Young people are at particular risk of becoming addicted. Alcohol is implicated in half of male suicides and over a quarter of female suicides in the former Soviet Union. The roots of much of Eastern European culture have long been steeped in alcohol, and heavy drinking is not considered problematic (in contrast with drug use). People drink anything from antifreeze to moonshine (an illegally produced distilled beverage). Venedict Yerofeyev's underground novel *Moscow to the End of the Line* describes a cocktail called 'Tears of a Komsomol Girl', containing eau-de-cologne, lemon soda, nail polish, lavender and mouthwash. (The Union of Communist Youth girl cries because the saboteurs and counter-revolutionaries are happy that all this patriotic production of health products—exceeding five-year-plan quotas!—is going to waste.)

Drug use was very heavily penalised under communism, but government controls have been relaxed or even disappeared, and the import and transit of illegal drugs has become much easier. Heroin from Afghanistan flows in abundance to the region through central Asia. The use of illicit drugs is growing fast, with injecting drug use playing an increasing role in transmitting HIV and hepatitis.

Alcohol consumption has reached alarming levels in Eastern Europe.

One consequence of the increasing use of psychoactive substances is the rapid and uncontrolled spread of HIV/AIDS. Injection is the main route of transmission. An estimated 1.7 million people in the region are living with HIV, of which 90% are in the Russian Federation and the Ukraine. This catastrophic figure represents an almost 20-fold increase in less than a decade. In the EU [European Union], the rates of reported newly diagnosed cases are mostly stable and low, or declining, but the HIV epidemic among IDUs [intravenous drug users] is growing in non-EU countries such as Azerbaijan, Belarus, Georgia, Kyrgyzstan, the Republic of Moldova, and Tajikistan.

This grim development raises the issue of a growth in 'triple diagnosis' of mental illness, substance abuse and HIV/ AIDS. The mental health problems associated with HIV are well documented: Mental illness and addictions increase vulnerability to infection, while being diagnosed with HIV/AIDS has profound effects on mental well-being through stigma and discrimination as well as the disease itself. Around three-quarters of people with HIV/AIDS will have at least one psychiatric disorder in their lifetime. Furthermore, mental health problems, drug and alcohol misuse, and learning difficulties can influence behaviour in ways that lead to greater risk of HIV infection. Populations particularly at risk—including IDUs, sex workers, migrants and prisoners—already have higher rates of mental illness than the general population.

Russia—The Sick Man of Europe

The average Russian man will die prematurely as a result of poor nutrition, smoking and binge drinking. Female Russians born in 2006 can expect to die nine years before their Western counterparts, while male Russians have a life expectancy of 59, which is 17 years less than Western Europeans. Nearly half of Russian men will die between the ages of 15 and 60, compared to 11% of German men and 9% of Japanese men.

Mental illness rates are soaring and suicide rates are extremely high, especially among men. Alcohol is implicated in half of male suicides and over a quarter of female suicides. . . .

Having for so long controlled attitudes, knowledge and treatment approaches to mental illness in Eastern Europe, mainly to their detriment, Russia now finds itself unable to respond effectively to these challenges. Its pattern is typical of, and in many cases worse than, its neighbours:

- high rates of mental illness, including the second-worst suicide rate in the world

- stigma and social exclusion

- outdated knowledge base

- minimal spending on mental health care

- huge treatment gap and inadequate services: primary health care deficiencies, warehouse-style asylums, few community-based services, human resources and medicines in short supply, no focus on intellectual disabilities, daily abuse of human rights

Jane Salvage and Rob Keukens,
"Tears of a Komsomol Girl: Perspectives
on Dual Diagnosis from Eastern Europe,"
Advances in Dual Diagnosis, *vol. 3, no. 3, August 2010, p. 6.*

Care and Treatment Responses

People with these coexisting problems face multiple stigmas and may have additional difficulties in accessing and adhering to treatment and care. . . . Few Eastern European countries have coherent policies to reduce drug and alcohol consumption, and implementation is patchy in those that do. Health and social care systems in the region cannot cope . . . and things could get worse before they get better. They are underfunded, poorly equipped and supplied, and lack professionals with adequate training, knowledge and expertise. Poor people often cannot afford to travel to clinics, pay the professionals (officially or under the table) or buy medication.

In Eastern Europe, people of all ages with developmental, mental or behavioural problems are isolated from others and from society, with few or no community-based services to help them maintain their treatment, reintegrate into society or find work. They are sometimes left in long-stay health or social care institutions for years, where their rights are routinely violated, and they have little or no say in their treatment or discharge.

The number of adequately trained mental health workers (whether psychiatrists, psychologists, nurses or social workers) is insufficient to meet the needs. Their training, where it exists, is usually out of date and there is very little continuing education. Health professional responses are strongly determined by the reductionist medical bias of their training, and they lack knowledge of addiction and its social-psychological dimensions, harm reduction and primary health care interventions. They are often fatalistic and describe patients in terms of their shortcomings, bringing few positive expectations and making negative moral judgments (as shown in both case studies). Addiction clinics mostly focus on detoxification with the goal of complete abstinence, although their expectations of success are very low.

The notion is slowly gaining ground that people with a dual or triple diagnosis need integrated, tailor-made services, but this has not led to solid government initiatives. There is little or no co-operation between psychiatric institutions, primary health care, social services and voluntary organisations, and most self-help and user groups are still in their infancy. Access to treatment of any kind is rare to nonexistent for HIV-positive, injecting drug users. All these problems are even more evident in services (or lack of them) for people in settings such as prisons.

The number of adequately trained mental health workers (whether psychiatrists, psychologists, nurses or social workers) is insufficient to meet the needs.

Problems and Solutions

Bleak as this picture is, there are some bright spots. One is the huge decline in the political abuse of psychiatry, thanks to the vigilance of dedicated human rights activists. Another is the growing determination among citizens—including people with mental health problems, their families, and reform-minded professionals—to transform mental health services and social attitudes. A range of projects, often with external support and funding, is reconfiguring services, letting fresh air and fresh ideas into closed institutions, developing networks, rewriting repressive legislation, updating training curricula and starting to put the person with mental health needs at the centre of planning and service delivery.

The growing interest in mental health issues worldwide provides an important stimulus. The World Health Organization devoted its 2001 world health report to mental illness and most Eastern European governments signed up to the declaration and action plan agreed at the World Health Organization European ministerial conference on mental health.

The European Union is developing mental health policies and networks, and is beginning to support mental health projects.

Further east, financial support for such work is thin and increasingly hard to obtain. Sadly, mental health development is itself stigmatised by most donors, who have invested little despite the scale of the problems. Progress is painfully slow. In most countries, reform efforts have started not with the policy makers but with a few brave service users, families and professionals.

Nongovernmental organisations (NGOs) have been founded to tackle mental health needs, many started by the mothers and wives of people with mental illness or learning disabilities to provide support services such as day centres and self-help groups. There are far too few of these and they often find themselves in conflict with uninterested or even hostile policy makers and public service leaders. Yet NGOs like Bemoni in Georgia, Somato in Moldova, and Mental Health and Society [Initiative] in Kyrgyzstan provide inspiring examples of what can be achieved, as well as initiatives like the three-year Cherkassy project in the Ukraine, financed by the Dutch Ministry of Foreign Affairs, which introduced new approaches to the prevention of psychoactive substance abuse.

Sadly, mental health development is itself stigmatised by most donors, who have invested little despite the scale of the problems.

Reform will require many more funded initiatives to foster significant shifts in attitude and culture, greater knowledge, full collaboration between services, multidisciplinary teamwork and user involvement—all the ingredients necessary to create a modern, ethical, client-oriented care system. Just as importantly, the powerful negative influence of the breakdown of social networks, communities and families throughout the region must be tackled, in a revival of the community spirit damaged or destroyed by poverty, civil war, migration, corruption and the loss of traditional attitudes, practices and cultures that helped people to cope with hardship.

The human toll of change in Eastern Europe is huge, but so far no government or international agency has risen fully to the task of visualizing a realistic future and way ahead for health systems, and providing the necessary political will and resources to make change happen. Drastic, structured measures are required, rather than crisis management through ad hoc policy measures and short-term programmes. The issue of dual diagnosis should be moved up the agenda, not least because young people, and thus the future social capital of the region, are at stake. We make some recommendations below.

Mental health has never been a priority: The tremendous task facing Eastern Europe requires huge efforts now and for the foreseeable future. Initiatives to create civil society, promote social inclusion and build capacity will all be crucial in tackling dual diagnosis, while the implications for policy and practice extend far beyond the traditional boundaries of health services.

Recommendations for Tackling Dual Diagnosis Problems

- Assess awareness, expertise and training needs of health and social care services (state and nongovernmental) that provide dual diagnosis care and treatment, as a foundation for developing programmes and strengthening referral networks.

- Provide training for primary and secondary health and social care staff in the recognition, prevention and treatment of dual diagnosis. Service users should be involved in the planning and provision of training.

- Identify existing materials for training, education and self-help, and adapt and translate these into local languages for local use, with development of new materials based on needs assessment.

- Expand services including counselling, psychosocial support groups, treatment of substance use, psychological and psychiatric assessment and treatment, self-help resources and social interventions such as occupational training.

- Strengthen community awareness by establishing partnerships and networking with a range of stakeholders in primary care, hospitals, prisons, community groups, schools, mental health user and carer groups, the media and policy makers.

- Address stigma and discrimination at policy and practice levels, including public education and awareness campaigns.

Periodical and Internet Sources Bibliography

The following articles have been selected to supplement the diverse views presented in this chapter.

Paul Armentano	"Study Debunks Claim That Pot Smoking Causes Mental Illness," *NORML Blog*, July 1, 2009. http://blog.norml.org.
Jonathan Campion, Ken Checinski, Jo Nurse, and Ann McNeill	"Smoking by People with Mental Illness and Benefits of Smoke-Free Mental Health Services," *Advances in Psychiatric Treatment*, 2008.
European Confederation of Primary Care Paediatricians	"Alcohol: Western and Eastern European Young People Develop Similar Drinking Patterns," November 23, 2010. http://ecpcp.eu.
David W. Freeman	"Psychosis Triggered by Smoking Pot? Marijuana Study Says Yes," CBS News, February 8, 2011.
Nady el-Guebaly	"Concurrent Substance-Related Disorders and Mental Illness: The North American Experience," *World Psychiatry*, vol. 3, no. 3, 2004.
National Alliance on Mental Illness	"Dual Diagnosis: Substance Abuse and Mental Illness," 2011. www.nami.org.
National Institute on Drug Abuse	"Topics in Brief: Comorbid Drug Abuse and Mental Illness," October 2007. www.drugabuse.gov.
Randeep Ramesh	"Substance Abuse, Not Mental Illness, Causes Violent Crime," *Guardian*, September 6, 2010.
SANE Australia	"Smoking and Mental Illness," 2012. www.sane.org.

CHAPTER 4

Mental Illness and Treatment

In Singapore, Treatment of Mental Illness Is Improving

Siow-Ann Chong

Siow-Ann Chong is senior consultant psychiatrist and vice chairman of the medical board of the Institute of Mental Health in Singapore. In the following viewpoint, he says that Singapore's mental health care system has been inadequate and ineffectual. He blames these failings on stigma against mental illness and on a lack of resources devoted to mental illness. He asserts, however, that Singapore has begun to take steps toward reform. He says that with continued attention and much work, Singapore's mental health system can improve.

As you read, consider the following questions:

1. According to the author, what is the psychiatrist-to-population ratio in Singapore, and how does it compare to other developed countries?
2. Why is psychiatry the most difficult and complex branch of medicine, according to the viewpoint?
3. Name one of the recommendations of Singapore's National Mental Health Blueprint for 2007–2010.

Siow-Ann Chong, "Mental Health in Singapore: A Quiet Revolution?," *Annals*, vol. 36, no. 10, October 2007, pp. 795–796. Copyright © 2007 by Annals, Academy of Medicine, Singapore (AAMS). All rights reserved. Reproduced by permission.

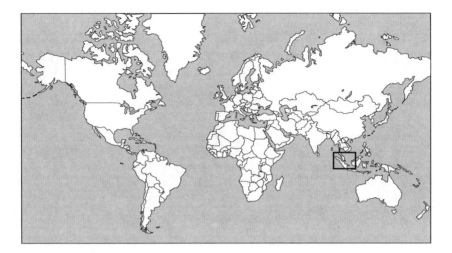

Worldwide there are about 450 million individuals in all societies who, in their lifetime, will suffer from a neuropsychiatric disorder that would exact a high toll in productivity and costs, and present serious health challenges (including death). This situation will get worse: The global burden of disease attributable to neuropsychiatric disorders is expected to rise from 12.3% in 2000 to 14.7% in 2020, with depression being the second most common cause of disability. The effect of major depression on quality of life is as great, or greater than, that of chronic medical conditions.

Mental Health Care Deficiencies in Singapore

A 2004 study in Singapore reported a lifetime prevalence of depression among adults as 5.6%, and that of dementia among the elderly as 5.2%. Not only do more people in Singapore die from suicide than from road traffic accidents every year, but conditions like schizophrenia, major depression, and alcohol-use disorders significantly increase the risk of early mortality.

Until recently, the responsibility for the care of people with mental illness in Singapore rested almost entirely with the specialised services in both the public and private sectors, complemented and supplemented by voluntary welfare organisations (VWOs). However, there has been a lack of coordination between the different medical and social services, which sometimes have conflicting and competing agendas. There was also a distinct lack of involvement of family physicians in public mental health care. A substantial proportion of people relied on a mixture of Western and traditional medicines, or used Western medicine only as a last resort. Cultural and religious beliefs often prompted patients to turn to the practitioners of traditional medicine or spiritual healers.

There are about 115 practising psychiatrists in Singapore, giving a psychiatrist-to-population ratio of about 2.6 per 100,000, which is low compared with other developed countries like the USA (13.7 per 100,000), the UK [United Kingdom] (11 per 100,000), and Australia (14 per 100,000). There is also a shortage across the whole slew of mental health professionals: psychiatric nurses, clinical psychologists, psychiatric case managers, medical social workers and occupational therapists.

More people in Singapore die from suicide than from road traffic accidents every year.

The financial coverage under the present health care system stresses on individual responsibility; it is based on a system of compulsory medical savings accounts and market forces. This system puts people with mental illness at a disadvantage and results in disparity of medical coverage.

The causes of most mental illnesses like autism, schizophrenia, bipolar disorder, obsessive-compulsive disorder are still unknown, so primary prevention is not possible. Some of these illnesses also strike early in one's life—before the individual can join the workforce, and the resulting disabilities may lead to academic and vocational impairment with consequent chronic financial difficulties. Employers often discriminate against mentally ill people. Research has established that mentally ill people are at a significantly higher risk of having lower educational attainment, living in poverty and a lower socioeconomic status.

Many mentally ill people in Singapore do not have Medi-save accounts, and MediShield excludes those with mental illnesses and personality disorders, leaving many to rely solely on Medifund (a default support mechanism).[1] Not surprisingly, patients at the Institute of Mental Health, the only state mental institute and Singapore's largest provider of mental health care, receive proportionately the most Medifund across all the restructured hospitals. To my knowledge, there is no private medical insurance company that provides cover for mental illness.

Stigma and Money

There are a number of reasons for this sorry state. Throughout history, stigma has clung tenaciously to mental illness, and among its various consequences, it prevents people with mental illness from studying, working and socialising in their community. Stigma makes the public less willing to pay for mental health care. It makes the public fearful—many believing that all people with mental illness are dangerous and should be locked away. This stigma also tinges the mental health professionals.

As the pathogenesis and pathophysiology of many mental disorders are still unknown, it makes mental health care vulnerable to perception that it is "not so scientific". We have yet to understand the biological substrates underlying some of the most simple and basic cognitions and emotions, let alone love, hate and fear. While psychiatry is arguably the "most humanistic discipline within medicine", our ignorance from the

1. Medisave is a national health care savings scheme in Singapore. MediShield is a medical insurance plan. Medifund is an endowment fund to pay medical costs for needy Singapore citizens.

mechanistic standpoint also makes it more uncertain, difficult and complex than any other branch of medicine.

Money—whether we like it or not—may be another factor. Although difficult to verify, the monetary remuneration that psychiatrists get is generally thought to be lower than that of other medical specialists. All these factors conspire to make psychiatry unattractive as a specialty of choice.

The level of mental health research activity varies between the various psychiatric centres in Singapore. Most of these centres are almost wholly service oriented. While there is some collaboration between the respective centres with other non-psychiatric disciplines, there is hardly any collaboration between the psychiatric centres: each centre operating within its own silo. The impact of these research activities on actual clinical care is not evident, and there is very little research to date that will help shape public policies on mental health.

Mental illness and mental health have traditionally been neglected topics for most governments. Data collected by the WHO [World Health Organization] showed the large gap that exists between resources that are available in countries for mental health and the burden caused by mental health problems.

Improvements in Mental Health Care

But things have started to change in Singapore. In 2005, the Ministry of Health tasked a committee of policy makers and mental health professionals to formulate the first National Mental Health Blueprint for the years 2007 to 2010. After deliberation, the committee articulated a number of recommendations which in essence aim to (a) build resilience to mental illness, (b) work towards early detection, (c) reduce stigma, (d) engage the primary care physicians and build up a network of support in the community, (e) rectify the shortfall in mental health workers, (f) encourage research, and finally to (g) develop a monitoring and evaluation system.

In principle, the blueprint proposes a population-based public health model, which is characterised by concern for the health of a population, and focuses also on the epidemiologic surveillance of the health of this population, on health promotion, disease prevention, and access to and evaluation of services. These goals are lofty and worthy but as always the devil will be in the details.

If we get our act together and work together . . . we can begin this journey to reform our mental health care system.

Clinician champions—in partnership with policy makers—have been appointed to drive the various initiatives. This is an enlightened measure. An article in the *Lancet* on the role of clinician leaders stresses their importance as "significant change in clinical domains cannot be achieved without the co-operation and support of the clinicians" and emphasises that there must be mutual understanding between these clinicians and policy makers. The policy makers must be cognizant of the way clinicians think, and appreciate what they value in their service to their patients; they must also curb their impatience to see overnight changes and instead accept incremental improvements. Correspondingly, the clinicians must be sensitive to the agenda of the policy makers—the financial and resource constraints, political expectations, and the need to show tangible results.

There is no doubt that much rests on the shoulders of these clinician leaders who must demonstrate clear-headed leadership and managerial abilities. They must break out of that parochial way of working within the silos of their respective organisations. They must also galvanise their fellow clinicians. They must be prepared to be held accountable and must articulate meaningful and actionable indicators by which their respective programmes would be evaluated.

What can be achieved also depends on other social, political and cultural forces. This first policy and blueprint will not address all the ills in the system—dealing with discriminatory employment policies and the disparity in medical coverage would require legislation, but it is for Singapore as good a start as any. If we get our act together and work together, and if we commit ourselves to matching our declarations with our actions, and our ambitions with outcomes, we can begin this journey to reform our mental health care system.

In Canada, Providing the Mentally Ill with Housing Can Aid Them in Recovery

Canadian Mental Health Association (Ontario)

The Canadian Mental Health Association (CMHA) in Ontario is a charitable organization that works to improve the lives of people with mental illness and their families. In the following viewpoint, CMHA says that mental illness is often linked to homelessness; the mentally ill often become homeless and homelessness contributes to stress, depression, and mental illness. CMHA argues that providing affordable housing and support services to the mentally ill can help them recover and substantially improve their health. CMHA maintains that housing for the mentally ill is also economical, since it reduces expensive psychiatric hospital stays.

As you read, consider the following questions:

1. According to CMHA, to what does adequate, suitable, and affordable housing lead?

2. According to CMHA, an Ontario study measuring participants' hospital use before and after a supportive housing intervention showed what results?

196

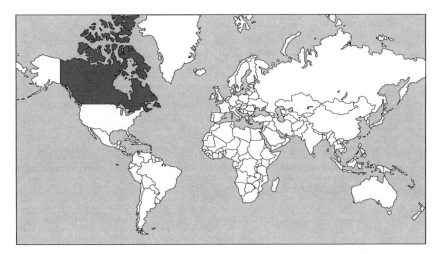

3. How much does CMHA say it costs to keep a person in a psychiatric hospital, and how does this compare to the cost of housing a person in the community with supports?

Housing is a basic human right and requirement for good health. When housing is inadequate or unavailable, individual as well as community well-being may suffer. The high cost of rental accommodations and home ownership has created a critical shortage of affordable housing and is a leading contributor to poverty in Ontario.

Housing Facts

According to the United Nations the right to housing is protected under international law and Canada has endorsed such rights guaranteeing "an adequate standard of living . . . including adequate food, clothing and housing." Likewise, the Ottawa Charter for Health Promotion identifies shelter as a basic prerequisite for health.

Adequate, suitable and affordable housing contributes to our physical and mental well-being. It leads to increased personal safety and helps decrease stress, leading to improved sleep and diet. All of these factors result in better mental health outcomes.

Affordable housing is an investment in health promotion and illness prevention.

Adequate dwellings are defined as those not requiring any major repairs, whereas suitable dwellings refer to those that have enough bedrooms for the size of the household. Accommodations are considered to be affordable if they cost less than 30 percent of the total pre-tax household income.

Affordable housing is an investment in health promotion and illness prevention. When a person has adequate housing, they experience fewer health problems and are able to devote more of their income to adequately feed and clothe themselves and their family.

Social housing:

- As of 2011, Ontario has
  - 260,000 public housing units
  - 41,454 cooperative housing units
  - 223,885 nonprofit housing units
  - 2,201 urban native housing units
  - 11,317 supportive housing units [a combination of housing and services for people with mental illness, addiction, or other health issues] (as of 2010)

- At the beginning of 2011, there were 152,077 low-income households on active waiting lists for social housing in Ontario.

- Applicants often wait several years before they are placed in housing.

Supportive housing:

- Ontario has 10,376 supportive housing units for people with mental illness (as of 2010).

- Wait lists for supportive housing range from 1 to 6 years, depending on the region.

Housing and Mental Illness

For people with serious mental illnesses, a safe and affordable home can be a place to live in dignity and move toward recovery. In fact, individuals with serious mental illness frequently identify income and housing as the most important factors in achieving and maintaining their health. However, for many, maintaining safe and affordable housing can be difficult. During periods of illness, individuals may be unable to work and/or experience a loss of income. Without adequate income, they may have difficulty paying rent and may eventually lose their household contents and their home. Consequently, many live in substandard housing that is physically inadequate, crowded, noisy and located in undesirable neighborhoods.

Two trends are largely responsible for the rise in homelessness over the past 15–20 years: a growing shortage of affordable rental housing and a simultaneous increase in poverty.

Homelessness and poverty are linked. Poor people are frequently unable to pay for housing, food, child care, health care and education. Difficult choices must be made when limited resources cover only some of these necessities. Being poor means being an illness, an accident or a paycheque away from living on the streets.

What Constitutes Homelessness?

- Persons who reside in places that are not intended as, or are unfit for, human habitation, including cars, abandoned buildings, bus or train stations, under bridges, in garbage or recycling dumpsters, parks, or other places lacking basic amenities.

- Persons sharing housing at the whim of other persons on an interim or emergency basis.

- Persons whose primary nighttime . . . abode is a supervised publicly or privately operated shelter designed to provide temporary living accommodations, including shelters for victims of domestic violence, welfare hotels, congregate shelters and transitional housing.

Two trends are largely responsible for the rise in homelessness over the past 15–20 years: a growing shortage of affordable rental housing and a simultaneous increase in poverty.

It is difficult to state whether homelessness or mental illness occurs first. Each case must be considered individually. Research tends to support both theories. The stress of being homeless may exacerbate previous mental illness. However, the difficulties of being homeless may encourage anxiety or depressive disorders.

Poverty is common among many persons with mental illness, which increases the risk of homelessness. The challenge of providing stable housing for persons with serious mental illness is reflected in the estimated 67 percent of homeless persons with a lifetime history of mental illness in Toronto.

People with serious mental illness are disproportionately affected by homelessness. The consequences of homelessness tend to be more severe when coupled with mental illness. People with mental illnesses remain homeless for longer periods of time and have less contact with family and friends. They encounter more barriers to employment and tend to be in poorer health than other homeless people.

Homelessness and Mental Illness in Sweden

In Sweden, . . . an individual perspective [on homelessness] dominated for a long time, and homelessness has been mainly analysed and explained with reference to individual factors such as substance abuse and dependence, mental disabilities or other social problems; if these problems disappear then it should also be possible to solve the problem of homelessness. Gradually, however, this explanation has changed. . . . A multifactorial explanatory model has been adopted in its place, where structural factors like the structure of the housing market are of vital importance. . . . One of the fundamental ideas of . . . [such new approaches] is to separate treatment from housing. This renders the structural and individual factors visible, and it becomes clear that homelessness is much more than just an individual problem.

Annika Remaeus and Ann Jönsson,
"Review: Sam Tsemberis (2010), Housing First Manual:
The Pathways Model to End Homelessness for People with Mental
Illness and Addiction," European Journal of Homelessness,
vol. 5, no. 2, December 2011, p. 235.

Types of Housing and Benefits

There are many housing options available to people living with serious mental illness.

Supportive housing is often communal in nature with a small number of tenants. Support services are provided on-site with 24-hour access to case management, emergency response and homemaking. Rehabilitation is the primary focus. It is frequently transitional housing, meant to prepare people for more independent living.

Supported housing involves individuals living in affordable housing of their choice that is indistinguishable from others in the neighbourhood. Supports are individualized to a person's needs and independent from the housing itself. Community integration and rehabilitation are encouraged. Supported housing is considered a best practice model and has demonstrated positive outcomes in community residency, satisfaction and quality of life.

Both supportive and supported housing promote recovery and independence, keeping people healthy and out of the hospital. For example, an Ontario study measuring participants' hospital use before and after a supportive housing intervention showed that all 34 residents in the study reduced their mean hospital days from 53.4 to 0.53 after one year.

A stable and supported living environment is essential to maintaining the health and well-being of people with serious mental illness and is integral to their recovery.

For those with a serious mental illness who can live independently in the community, poverty is a major barrier to acquiring housing. *Rent supplements* or *rent-geared-to-income* housing are strategies that provide individuals with the financial resources they need to access desirable housing in their community. Research shows that personal choice in housing not only increases citizens' housing stability, but also helps to improve well-being and quality of life.

Research indicates that a stable and supported living environment is essential to maintaining the health and well-being of people with serious mental illness and is integral to their recovery. Housing with support can generate positive outcomes, including enhanced life skills, improved health status, an increased sense of empowerment and involvement in the community. Research shows that maintaining and improving the housing of individuals with serious mental illness can contribute to a reduction in psychiatric symptoms and therefore decrease the need for emergency and treatment services.

Community mental health services can assist people to both access and maintain their housing. Some of the key supports that have been identified by people with serious mental illness include medical services available in-house or on-call (for crisis management and medication monitoring), homemaking and personal care services, vocational training, lifeskills training, as well as assistance with income support and housing advocacy. Service providers have also identified the following factors which support successful housing arrangements: rent geared to income, community support services, a strong personal support network, and availability of case management.

Improvements in housing quality lead to better mental health outcomes for residents. Investing in housing quality often involves major refurbishing and can lead to greater satisfaction, feelings of safety and increased community involvement. Neighbourhoods can also have a significant impact on the success of housing for people with mental illness by contributing to an individual's ability to feel comfortable and integrated within the community.

Affordable and Supportive Housing Makes Economic Sense

Affordable housing makes economic sense. Many factors contribute to a city's economic success, such as the talent of its residents, location, transportation and government investment. Affordable housing is also part of this equation, enabling employees to live in a community. As TD Economics [a Canadian-based bank group] states, "... working to find solutions to the problem of affordable housing is also smart economic policy. An inadequate supply of housing can be a major impediment to business investment and growth."

Likewise, supportive housing is economical. It costs approximately $486 a day ($177,390 per year) to keep a person in a psychiatric hospital, compared to $72 per day ($26,280 per year) to house a person in the community with supports.

Furthermore, persons who cannot afford to live in decent housing are more likely to experience exposure to violence, communicable diseases and increased chronic conditions.

The challenges of poverty, stigma and discrimination that persons with mental illness face directly impact their ability to access, find and keep housing. In 2006, 77,430 people with a mental illness received income support from the Ontario Disability Support Program (ODSP), comprising 35 percent of the caseload. In Ontario, the average market rent for a one-bedroom apartment ranges from $453 to $896. However, the maximum shelter allowance for a single person receiving ODSP is $436. Thus, persons in receipt of income support face an increased risk of becoming homeless.

Due to stigma, the typical reaction encountered by someone with a mental illness is fear and rejection. Many living with a mental illness are often denied housing in the private market as a result of their psychiatric illness.

Furthermore, many supportive housing projects also encounter a "not-in-my-backyard" response (NIMBYism) from neighbours, businesses, councillors, etc. This type of behaviour may include discriminating and slandering comments in person, by e-mail, or through flyers and posters which protest a new supportive housing development.

Despite improvements in Ontario's economy and a modest level of rental development in a number of markets, there continues to be a serious housing affordability issue in Ontario. There are fewer affordable housing units available now than a decade ago. Since 1995, there has been a net loss of 13,000 affordable housing units in Ontario.

CMHA Ontario is active in supporting persons with mental illness to access adequate, safe and affordable housing. We do this by advocating for more affordable housing, supportive housing, community supports and rent supplements.

We are also involved in promoting mental health through highlighting public issues and recommending options to create inclusive and supportive environments.

In South Africa, Mental Health Treatment Should Be Incorporated into Care for HIV/AIDS

Khopotso Bodibe

Khopotso Bodibe is a journalist for the Cape Town–based news agency Health-e. In the following viewpoint, he reports that mental health conditions are growing quickly among people in South Africa who are infected with HIV/AIDS. He reports that this is in part because people with mental illnesses are more likely to engage in behaviors that cause them to contract HIV, and partly because HIV can affect mental functioning either through brain infection or stress brought on by the disease. Bodibe says that the health care establishment in South Africa needs to make a greater effort to incorporate mental health services into HIV treatment.

As you read, consider the following questions:

1. According to Melvyn Freeman, what percentage of South Africans suffer from some form of mental illness, and how does this compare to the percentage of those with HIV/AIDS who suffer from mental illness?

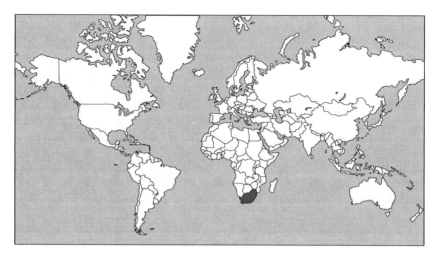

2. What did researchers find out about the relationship between risk behavior and depression?

3. According to Rita Thom, what are the three groups of mental health conditions that affect people with HIV/ AIDS?

People living with HIV and AIDS are at an increased risk of developing serious mental disorders, according to mental health professionals at a Johannesburg [a city in South Africa] meeting this week [in September 2010].

The Relationship Between Mental Illness and AIDS

The meeting resolved that mental health interventions should be incorporated into existing AIDS services.

Studies from all over the world show that mental health disorders are growing fast among people infected with HIV compared to the general population. People with HIV have double the incidence of mental illnesses of HIV-negative people. Cluster manager of the Non-Communicable Diseases Unit in the National Department of Health, Professor Melvyn Freeman, was involved in a study that showed similar results in 2007.

"In the general population it was found that South Africa has 16.5% of people suffering from some form of mental disorder. When you come to people living with HIV, it went up to 43.7%. That's a huge difference", Prof Freeman said.

"When you look at the higher rates among HIV-infected people, you have to ask the question: Is this because they had a prior condition and their vulnerability led to their infection or is it that, because they have contracted HIV, it has a mental impact on them, and, therefore, this raises the numbers of people living with HIV who have mental disorders. This is a complex issue and I would like to suggest that both are true that it's very, very likely that mental disorder is both a risk factor and a consequence of HIV", he continued.

Quoting a study conducted among school-going youths in KwaZulu-Natal [a province in South Africa], Freeman supported the theory that having a mental disorder is a risk factor for contracting HIV.

"It's very, very likely that mental disorder is both a risk factor and a consequence of HIV."

"They looked, initially, at the relationship between knowledge of HIV and risk behaviour. . . . Not surprisingly, from what we know, there was very little correlation between knowledge of HIV and risk behaviour. They also measured these youths' depression and not surprisingly, in my view, they found that those who had higher levels of depression had higher risk behaviours.[1] That makes sense to me because if you don't really care about your life and your future, are you really going to take the protection that you should be taking? So, depression, then, for me, is a key risk factor for contracting HIV. Having a mental disorder—whether it's a serious

---

1. HIV can be transmitted sexually or by intravenous drug use, so risk behaviours would include unprotected sex or sharing needles.

mental disorder or a more common mental disorder, such as depression—the risk factor is higher".

Freeman also showed how a mental health disorder can be a result of having HIV.

"We have to look at the other side. What does it feel like to actually be told that you have HIV? How do you cope with this? Who do you tell? Who don't you tell? How are you going to be accepted? People living with HIV have informed me that this is a real, real difficult thing to handle and if you do not have support, and if you do not have help to get through this initial period and as you have to live longer with HIV, it does become a difficult thing to live with".

"They are dying. And they are dying because all of us in this room, operating in this field, we have actually not invested enough time."

HIV and Three Types of Mental Disorders

Professor Rita Thom, a psychiatrist with more than 30 years of experience, added that from a medical perspective, it's not uncommon for people living with HIV to acquire a mental health condition. She said these mental health conditions can be divided into three groups.

"That is the HIV-associated neuropsychiatric disorders. Those are the disorders that result from HIV brain infection; then you've got HIV and serious mental illness, which is quite complicated because it includes both some of the results of HIV brain infection as well as people who have a primary psychiatric disorder and then become HIV infected; and, then, there is a very large group of people who have HIV and what we call common mental disorders, which are depression, anxiety, substance use disorders", said Prof Thom.

Deputy Minister of Public Works, Hendrietta Bogopane-Zulu, attended the meeting. She expressed concern that it has

Mental Illness, Substance Abuse, and HIV/AIDS in South Africa

People living with HIV/AIDS experience psychological distress throughout the duration of the HIV disease. More than half of people newly diagnosed with HIV present with psychiatric conditions, most often clinical depression and post-traumatic stress. Alcohol use is also common to people living with HIV/AIDS. The experience of being diagnosed with a life-threatening illness, particularly a highly stigmatised condition like HIV/AIDS, undoubtedly underlies many of the mental health problems observed in HIV-infected people. However, negative affective conditions such as depression and anxiety, as well as alcohol and drug use, probably existed prior to testing HIV positive for many people living with HIV/AIDS. In fact, depression, substance use, and maladaptive coping are among the more reliable predictors of HIV risk behaviour and should not be expected to dissipate when a person tests positive for HIV. These mental health conditions should therefore be addressed in positive prevention interventions. Indeed, research has shown that the effectiveness of positive prevention interventions in reducing HIV transmission risks may at least in part be accounted for by reductions in co-occurring emotional distress.

Seth C. Kalichman and Mark Lurie,
"Positive Prevention Interventions," HIV/AIDS in South Africa,
2nd edition, Eds. S.S. Abdool Karim and Q. Abdool Karim,
New York: Cambridge University Press, 2010, p. 264.

taken the mental health service provider community too long to articulate themselves on the issue even when the inextricable link between mental health illness and HIV was evident for many years.

"Those in the forefront of mental health have actually not rolled up their sleeves and taken up the fight. Three weeks ago I've gone to three funerals of women with mental disabilities in the former Transkei. They are dying. And they are dying because all of us in this room, operating in this field, we have actually not invested enough time. And a lot of people with mental illness that are supposed to be on ARVs [antiretroviral drugs, or anti-AIDS drugs] are not on ARVs", she said.

As the current national strategic plan on HIV and AIDS is coming to an end, mental health professionals resolved that they need to organize themselves to lobby for the recognition of mental health and HIV and AIDS as co-morbidities whose treatment approaches must be integrated in the next national strategic plan.

In Argentina, a Treatment Program Providing Companionship for the Mentally Ill Has Been Successful

Marcela Valente

Marcela Valente is the Inter Press Service correspondent in Argentina, specializing in social and gender issues. In the following viewpoint, she reports on a program in Argentina in which jobless people are hired as companions to spend time with discharged mental patients. Valente says that the companions are given training, but not psychiatric training. Instead, she explains they are simply expected to visit with and be available for people with mental illnesses, reporting any problems to professionals. Valente says the program has been a major success in improving quality of life for the mentally ill and has also cut costs by substantially reducing psychiatric admissions.

As you read, consider the following questions:

1. How many patients have used the mental health home companionship program, according to Valente, and from what sorts of conditions were they suffering?

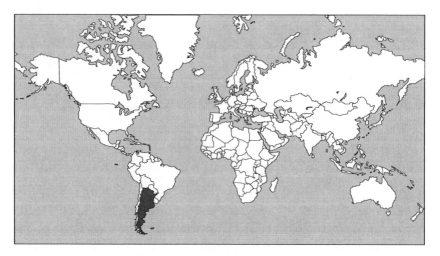

2. According to Valente, what is the duration of companionship training?

3. What examples does Gladys Mamani give of things she does for her clients in her role as a companion?

An innovative mental health plan developed in a town in the Argentine province of La Pampa has reduced to a minimum relapses among patients discharged from hospital, while at the same time providing new and valued employment for jobless people living on state subsidies.

Supporting Patients

The mental health home companionship programme began 14 years ago [in 1994], as an initiative of the professional team serving acute psychiatric patients at the Gobernador Centeno Hospital in General Pico, a town of 60,000 in the north of La Pampa, 600 kilometres northwest of Buenos Aires.

"We had 16 beds, for acute psychiatric patients only, within the general hospital," social worker Cristina Proia told IPS [Inter Press Service news agency].

"We saw that they were staying in hospital for three or four months, which is a long time for an acute patient, and after they were discharged they would relapse," she said.

So an alternative way to support patients in the community and prevent new admissions was devised. The team of health professionals interviewed about 25 unemployed people who were receiving a government subsidy, and selected eight who were given training to provide companionship to discharged patients.

"We try to work with the patient's healthy side. It's not useful for us to know about his or her diagnosis or about the medication. We just provide companionship," Gladys Mamani, a woman who was unemployed and joined the programme 11 years ago and whose experience now qualifies her to work in public and private health care, told IPS.

Proia, who works alongside psychologist Ana Viglianco and other professionals, says that over 100 patients have used the programme in the past 14 years. Among them were people suffering from different forms of psychosis or depression, and people at psychosocial risk such as low-income teenage mothers.

Many of the people in the programme are psychiatric outpatients who need support to ensure they take prescribed medication, and someone to alert health professionals about behaviour that may suggest a risk of relapse. But the programme also seeks to prevent people with mental problems who have not required hospital admission from developing a chronic illness.

"Among the unemployed people who showed interest in our project were some highly perceptive people whose vocation and skill became more clear as they worked with each patient," said Proia.

Companion Training

Initial training lasts less than two months, because theoretical instruction is not given. Essentially, the would-be companionship providers analyse and confront their prejudices.

"The basic training is for them to work on their preconceptions about madness, their feelings about the patients, and how to be committed to patients while preserving sufficient distance to really see and observe. We don't teach the companions about psychiatric profiles or medication, because the professionals see to that," she said.

Essentially [through training], the would-be companionship providers analyse and confront their prejudices.

The idea of the programme is that the companionship providers should "maintain a certain degree of naivety" which will help them detect changes in the patients' behaviour.

Health professionals then decide whether the behavioural change is a symptom that requires attention, and whether to adjust the patient's medication or readmit him or her for a day or two.

Each companionship provider looks after five or six patients, who call him or her whenever they feel the need.

They may be called at daily, weekly or monthly intervals, until the patient can manage independently. The health care team supervises the activity of the companionship providers on a daily basis.

"Only a few companionship providers misunderstood their role, and tried to tell the patients what they should do and how they should live, instead of providing support for the patients' needs. Most, on the other hand, have found paid employment in this work, even in the private health care system," said Proia, who added that the new focus is now widely accepted.

For instance, the family of a patient who was discharged six years ago offered to pay the companionship provider, who continues to be supervised by the state hospital, however.

At present there are only two companionship workers in the programme because of a lack of funds. Instead of the government subsidy they are now paid salaries out of the provincial public health budget.

"I hope this programme can continue with more funding, and that it can be developed in other places. If it were carried out at a national level, it would be extraordinary, because it would improve the quality of life of a great many patients. But of course, that would require strong political will," Proia said.

Reduced Costs, Improved Lives

She estimated that the number of psychiatric admissions in General Pico has fallen by 90 percent because of the programme. The average cost per patient is over 1,100 dollars a month. However, Proia said the main thing is not the potential cost reduction, but the improvement achieved in the lives of people with mental illness.

"The 'deinstitutionalisation' of mental patients is often talked about, but we say that alternative arrangements must be made so that they are not abandoned to their fate," she said. Not all the discharged patients have relatives willing or able to take them in, and mental conditions, to a greater or lesser degree, tend to be chronic.

"The point is you don't have to do anything for them, just be with them."

Having spent over a decade looking after children, teenagers, adults and elderly people, Mamani says that the core idea is simply being there. "For instance, I go to birthdays and other gatherings when I am invited, and often I'm the only person there who isn't part of the family, but to all of them I'm 'a friend.'" One might say she is "the" friend.

"Once I was out walking with a 30-year-old woman, and she asked me to sing nursery rhymes with her, and I did, although I knew that I looked ridiculous singing them. The point is you don't have to do anything for them, just be with them," she says, smiling.

The hardest times, on the other hand, are when the patients can't even talk, but she still knows that at some point they will connect. "Once I went into a darkened house where there was only silence and no one spoke, until after a while a voice said 'stay with me.' That's what this work is like," she said.

Mexico Needs to Improve Its Treatment of Mental Illness in Adolescents

G. Borges, C. Benjet, ME Medina-Mora, R. Orozco, and PS Wang

G. Borges, C. Benjet, and ME Medina-Mora are affiliated with the Instituto Nacional de Psiquiatria in Mexico; R. Orozco is affiliated with the Secretaría de Salud in Mexico City; and PS Wang is affiliated with the National Institute of Mental Health in Bethesda, Maryland. In the following viewpoint, the authors report that the large majority of adolescents with mental health problems in Mexico fail to receive adequate treatment. They say the failure to receive care may be the result of stigma associated with mental illness, lack of training among providers, or poverty and an inability to pay for care. They conclude that the situation is a crisis and that so many adolescents with untreated mental health issues may have serious long-term consequences for Mexican society.

As you read, consider the following questions:

1. What mental health disorder do the authors say had the highest level of treatment among adolescents?

Adapted by the publisher, with permission, from: G. Borges, C. Benjet, ME Medina-Mora, R. Orozco, and PS Wang, "Treatment of Mental Disorders for Adolescents in Mexico City," *Bulletin of the World Health Organization*, vol. 86, no. 10, October 2008, pp. 757–764. Copyright © 2008 by the World Health Organization. All rights reserved. Reproduced by permission.

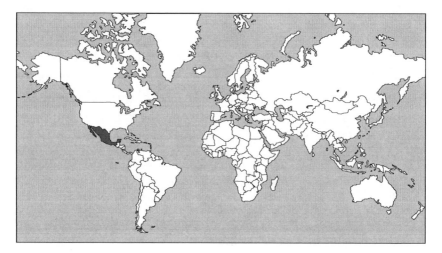

2. According to the authors, how many child psychiatric hospitals are there in Mexico, and where are they located?

3. Name a specific suggestion the authors make for improving mental health care among adolescents in Mexico.

In Mexico, as elsewhere, only a minority of adults with psychiatric disorders receive some form of treatment. However, it is unclear to what extent this situation is similar for Mexican adolescents. Some studies of adult populations have shown that younger adult cohorts are more likely to receive care than older cohorts. However, other studies, mostly conducted in developed countries, have begun to shed light on important shortfalls in the mental health care received by adolescents.

In 2001–2002, the National Institute of Psychiatry in Mexico conducted the Mexico National Comorbidity Survey, which is part of WHO's [World Health Organization's] World Mental Health Survey Initiative. Results for the urban Mexican adult population showed that fewer than one in five respondents with a 12-month prevalence of a psychiatric disorder used any service during the previous year and only one in every two respondents who used services received care that met minimal standards for adequacy. In 2005, the National Institute of Psychiatry in Mexico conducted the Mexican Adolescent Mental Health Survey employing similar methodology. We report here the rate of mental health service use in the previous year among these adolescents, the adequacy of treatments, and potential determinants of service use and treatment adequacy. . . .

Those attending school . . . had a significantly increased likelihood . . . of receiving adequate health care compared to those not attending school.

Results Among Adolescents in Mexico City

9.1% of the adolescents [surveyed] used any service for emotional problems, with a higher use of services among those with a disorder (13.7%) compared to those with no disorder (6.1%). Respondents with a substance use disorder reported the greatest use of services, and those with an anxiety disorder the lowest. For those with any disorder, the health care sector was the most widely used for mental health services (by 9.5%), with school-based treatments being next most frequent. Most services delivered by the health care sector were provided by mental health specialists, with minimal participation of the general medical sector. The disorder with the highest level of treatment was drug abuse with dependence (38%, largely treated in the non–health care system), followed by conduct disorder (25%, largely treated in the health care system). . . .

Among those with a psychiatric disorder, 80% used only one type of provider, 17% two types of providers, and 3% used three or more types of providers. Among those that used two providers, the most common combination was for health care and school-based providers. About 72% of those used both services simultaneously, while 18% used school services first and later reported the use of a health care provider. In the health care sector, the mean number of visits was 7.8 for those with a psychiatric disorder and 6.2 for those without a disorder; for the non–health care sector it was 19.1 and 16.5 visits respectively, and for school-based services it was 14.9 and 16.9 visits, respectively. . . .

Overall, 58.4% of those receiving any services obtained any treatment that could be considered minimally adequate, with anxiety disorders showing the lowest percentage and substance use disorders the highest. Those with a disorder were more likely to receive adequate treatment than those without a disorder and the health care sector showed the lowest level of adequacy. . . .

The greater likelihood of service use and adequacy of services for those attending school may be related to school-based programmes being exclusively available for this group only. For this reason, we refitted our models to obtain results for health care and non–health care services separately. In these analyses, respondents attending school were no more likely to get health care or non–health care services than those not attending school. Nevertheless, those attending school still had a significantly increased likelihood . . . of receiving adequate health care compared to those not attending school.

Reforms Are Needed

Less than one in seven adolescents with any psychiatric disorder in the last 12 months used any services. Although this is the first time that representative service use data are available for adolescents in Mexico, prior research among adults in Mexico also showed that the majority of people with a recent psychiatric disorder did not receive recent treatment. Comparable data from other developed countries confirms the large unmet need that adolescents face. A study of another Latino population in Puerto Rico showed that only 26% of adolescents affected by mental disorders used services. Our results reveal the even larger gap that adolescents in Mexico face, with only 14% of those with a disorder using any service in the prior 12 months. Data for comparison on service use in other Latin American countries are lacking, although the situation of scarce resources, as well as few services and personnel for treating children having a mental disorder, is commonplace in the region. The lack of resources in Mexico City may be similar to other less-developed countries, although more research is needed before we can generalize our findings. Respondents without a disorder comprised about 40% of the population using services, raising concern that scarce resources for mental health care may be misallocated. However, some services may be used by respondents with lifetime histories of disorders; other respondents without apparent disorders may also be using services appropriately for primary prevention, sub-threshold symptoms that do not qualify as full-blown disorders or for disorders not assessed by our survey.

Our results on the percentages receiving minimally adequate care (58%) as well as a more stringent definition (27%) are very low and similar to rates reported among adults in Mexico, suggesting that the entire system of care for mental disorders is in need of reform. The system for child mental health care in Latin America has been described as excessively focused on serious and rare disorders. A recent evaluation of psychiatric care in Mexico concluded that it is still mainly provided by large public psychiatric hospitals. Even though this study did not focus specifically on adolescents, these conclusions could well apply to youth.

Less than one in seven adolescents with any psychiatric disorder in the last 12 months used any services.

There are many potential reasons for failure to receive minimally adequate care. Individuals with mental disorders, especially those with the most serious and impairing forms, may suffer from considerable stigmatization and discrimination associated with their mental disorder and may lack the ability and resources to consistently access mental health treatments. Patients may also find prescribed treatments intolerable. Providers may lack the training to recognize and properly diagnose mental disorders or lack the knowledge concerning optimal treatment regimens. These results may not be surprising, given the dearth of mental health resources in Mexico. It is noteworthy that there is only one child psychiatric hospital in the entire country, located in Mexico City.

Two socio-demographic characteristics predicted the use of mental health services among subjects with psychiatric disorders, being female and having more educated parents. Some studies find adolescent males to be more likely to receive services than females, but others have failed to do so. It is not clear why in this Mexican sample, females with psychiatric disorders were more likely to get services, but it is possible that the Mexican culture, that emphasizes protection of young females more so than males, could play a role or that deviant behaviour is tolerated more in males than females. More educated parents may be more likely to recognize symptoms of distress and mental disorders in their child and be able to seek treatment. It is possible that these adolescents have more supportive environments or more assistance in promoting treatment adherence. Although Mexico is a country with low socioeconomic status and the lack of financial resources may help explain the low rate of service use, we did not find an association between income and receiving any treatment or minimally adequate treatment—a lack of association also reported from other studies in developed countries, but not all. . . .

An Enormous Public Health Problem

Improvement in the mental health care of Mexican youth is urgently needed and should not depend only on additional services and resources. Our results shed light on an enormous public health problem facing Mexico. The large majority of those with needs received no treatment from any sector. The negative public health consequences of such unmet needs for treatment in adolescents are likely to be large. In this context, the development of additional mental health resources is sorely needed and an essential first step. However, reallocation of services and providers will be needed to take advantage of the resources that are made available. Active outreach, school-based programmes employing brief screens may be needed for the accurate identification of children with mental disorders. Interventions to train non–health care professionals to recognize children with mental health conditions and make referrals for health care may also be useful. Finally, even among Mexican youth with mental disorders from families with financial means, addressing out-of-pocket costs and other economic barriers may also be critical for increasing the generally low intensity and widespread inadequacy of mental health treatments.

Periodical and Internet Sources Bibliography

The following articles have been selected to supplement the diverse views presented in this chapter.

Betty Ann Adam	"National Housing Study Shows Good Outcomes for Mentally Ill," *Vancouver Sun*, April 4, 2012.
BBC News	"Mental Health Nurses 'Set Bad Example to Patients,'" March 21, 2011.
CBC News	"Housing First for Mentally Ill Homeless," November 23, 2009.
Centro Cultural do Ministério da Saúde	"The Brazilian Psychiatric Reform and the Mental Health Policy," 2012. www.ccs.saude .gov.
Chang Ai-Lien	"'1 in 10 Will Suffer from Mental Illness': Study," *Strait Times* (Singapore), November 19, 2011.
IRIN	"Global: Governments 'Still Failing' on Mental Health Issues," October 18, 2011. www.irinnews.org.
Pamela J. Johnson	"Mexico Program Targets Care for Mentally Ill," USC News, January 23, 2012. http://news.usc.edu.
Beth Murphy	"The Mind Guide to Housing and Mental Health," Mind, 2011. www.mind.org.uk.
Kristin Palitza	"Health-South Africa: Mental Illness in HIV-Positive Patients Largely Ignored," Inter Press Service, June 8, 2009. http://ipsnews.net.
Marcela Valente	"Argentina: The Long Adios to Psychiatric Hospitals," Inter Press Service, March 17, 2011. http://ipsnews.net.

For Further Discussion

Chapter 1

1. Why does Metin Basoglu say that earthquake trauma is similar to torture trauma? Find evidence in the viewpoints by Julie R. Grier and Devin Powell that either supports or contradicts Basoglu's position.

2. Based on the viewpoints by IRIN and the *Daily Mirror*, what are some similarities between the mental health difficulties faced by Afghans and by British soldiers who served in Afghanistan? What are some differences?

Chapter 2

1. Why does Human Rights Watch see the high levels of incarceration in the United States as a human rights issue? In light of the treatment of mentally ill prisoners, do you agree that the incarceration rate is a human rights issue? Why or why not?

2. What evidence do Wan Yanhai and Yuri Savenko, in his interview with Vaughan Bell, present to show that China and Russia use mental hospitals to silence dissidents? Who do you think makes the strongest case against his respective government? Explain your answer.

Chapter 3

1. Based on your readings in this chapter, can cultural factors have an effect on substance abuse? Can cultural factors affect the prevalence of mental illness? Provide examples and explain your answers.

2. Based on the viewpoint by Deborah Cornah, do you think the ban on smoking will help or harm mentally ill patients in the United Kingdom? Explain your answer.

Chapter 4

1. G. Borges and his colleagues argue that Mexico needs to do much better in its mental health treatment of adolescents. Based on the other viewpoints in this chapter, what are some programs that might be implemented to help the mentally ill in Mexico?

Organizations to Contact

The editors have compiled the following list of organizations concerned with the issues debated in this book. The descriptions are derived from materials provided by the organizations. All have publications or information available for interested readers. The list was compiled on the date of publication of the present volume; the information provided here may change. Be aware that many organizations take several weeks or longer to respond to inquiries, so allow as much time as possible.

American Association of Suicidology (AAS)
5221 Wisconsin Avenue NW, Washington, DC   20015
(202) 237-2280 • fax: (202) 237-2282
e-mail: info@suicidology.org
website: www.suicidology.org

The American Association of Suicidology (AAS) is one of the largest suicide prevention organizations in the nation. It believes that suicidal thoughts are almost always a symptom of depression and that suicide is almost never a rational decision. AAS publishes the quarterly newsletter *Surviving Suicide*, the journal *Suicide and Life-Threatening Behavior*, and fact sheets.

Amnesty International
5 Penn Plaza, 14th Floor, New York, NY   10001
(212) 807-8400 • fax: (212) 463-9193
e-mail: aimember@aiusa.org
website: www.amnestyusa.org

Amnesty International is a worldwide movement of people who campaign for internationally recognized human rights. Its vision is of a world in which every person enjoys all of the human rights enshrined in the Universal Declaration of Human Rights and other international human rights standards. Each year it publishes a report on its work and its concerns throughout the world. Its website includes numerous reports and posts on mental illness and human rights issues, including "Isolated and Dehumanised: Inmates in Arizona's Isolation Units."

Canadian Mental Health Association (CMHA)

Phenix Professional Building, 595 Montreal Road, Suite 303
Ottawa, Ontario   K1K 4L2
  Canada
e-mail: info@cmha.ca
website: www.cmha.ca

The Canadian Mental Health Association (CMHA) is one of the oldest voluntary organizations in Canada. Its programs are designed to direct people suffering from mental illness to the help they need to cope with crises; regain confidence; and return to their communities, families, and jobs. The association publishes books, reports, policy statements, and pamphlets.

Department of Health, United Kingdom (DH)

Ministerial Correspondence and Public Enquiries Unit
Department of Health, Richmond House, 79 Whitehall
London   SW1A 2NS
  United Kingdom
020 7210 4850 • fax: 020 7210 5952
website: www.dh.gov.uk

The Department of Health of the United Kingdom is responsible for public health policy and for the National Health Service (NHS). It produces numerous reports, briefs, and fact sheets on mental illness, including "Attitudes to Mental Illness 2010 Research Report" and "Safety First: Five-Year Report of the National Confidential Inquiry into Suicide and Homicide by People with Mental Illness."

Human Rights Watch

350 Fifth Avenue, 34th Floor, New York, NY   10118-3299
(212) 290-4700 • fax: (212) 736-1300

e-mail: hrwnyc@hrw.org
website: www.hrw.org

Founded in 1978, Human Rights Watch is a nongovernmental organization that conducts systematic investigations of human rights abuses in countries around the world. It publishes many books and reports on specific countries and issues as well as annual reports and other articles. Its website includes numerous discussions of human rights and mental health issues, including "Letter to Peruvian Congress on Involuntary Detention of Persons with Disabilities" and "Keep Mentally Ill Out of Solitary Confinement."

International Foundation for Research and Education on Depression (iFred)

PO Box 17598, Baltimore, MD   21297-1598
(410) 268-0044 • fax: (443) 782-0739
e-mail: info@ifred.org
website: www.ifred.org

The International Foundation for Research and Education on Depression (iFred) is an organization dedicated to researching causes of depression, supporting those dealing with depression, and combating the stigma associated with depression. The foundation publishes a newsletter, and its website includes a blog, information about its projects, and fact sheets about depression.

Mental Health Council of Australia (MHCA)

PO Box 174, Deakin West   2600
   Australia
(02) 6285 3100 • fax: (02) 6285 2166
website: www.mhca.org.au

Mental Health Council of Australia (MHCA) is a national nongovernmental organization representing the Australian mental health sector. It promotes mental health for all Australians. The MHCA aims to promote mentally healthy communities, educate Australians on mental health issues, conduct research into mental health issues, and reform Australia's mental health system. It publishes the biweekly *MHCA Bulletin*, an occasional newsletter, and numerous fact sheets and reports, all of which are available on its website.

National Alliance on Mental Illness (NAMI)

3803 N. Fairfax Drive, Suite 100, Arlington, VA   22203
(703) 524-7600 • fax: (703) 524-9094
e-mail: info@nami.org
website: www.nami.org

The National Alliance on Mental Illness (NAMI) is a consumer advocacy and support organization composed largely of family members of people with severe mental illnesses such as schizophrenia, manic-depressive illness, and depression. The alliance adheres to the position that severe mental illnesses are biological brain diseases and that mentally ill people should not be blamed or stigmatized for their conditions. NAMI's publications include the magazine *NAMI Advocate*, published three times a year for members; the quarterly magazine *NAMI Beginnings* for parents and caregivers; the bilingual *Avanzamos* for the Latino community; the *NAMI Voice* for donors; and numerous newsletters.

National Institute of Mental Health (NIMH)

6001 Executive Boulevard, Room 8184, MSC 9663
Bethesda, MD   20892-9663
1-866-615-6464 • fax: (301) 443-4279
e-mail: nimhinfo@nih.gov
website: www.nimh.nih.gov/index.shtml

The National Institute of Mental Health (NIMH) is a scientific organization dedicated to research focused on the understanding, treatment, and prevention of mental disorders and the promotion of mental health. Its mission is to transform the understanding and treatment of mental illnesses through research to pave the way for prevention, recovery, and cure. Its website includes numerous fact sheets and discussions of mental illness. In addition, NIMH publishes booklets such as *Borderline Personality Disorder* and *Schizophrenia*.

World Health Organization (WHO)
525 Twenty-Third Street NW, Washington, DC   20037
(202) 974-3000 • fax: (202) 974-3663
e-mail: info@who.int
website: www.who.int

The World Health Organization (WHO) is an agency of the United Nations formed in 1948 with the goal of creating and ensuring a world where all people can live with high levels of both mental and physical health. WHO publishes the *Bulletin of the World Health Organization*, which is available online, and the *Pan American Journal of Public Health*. Its website includes numerous reports and discussions of mental health issues throughout the world, including "Mental Health Atlas 2011" and "Mental Health in Somalia."

Bibliography of Books

Jonathan D. Ablard

Madness in Buenos Aires: Patients, Psychiatrists, and the Argentine State, 1880–1983. Athens: Ohio University Press, 2008.

Metin Basoglu and Ebru Salcioglu

A Mental Healthcare Model for Mass Trauma Survivors: Control-Focused Behavioral Treatment of Earthquake, War, and Torture Trauma. New York: Cambridge University Press, 2011.

Michael B. Blank and Marlene M. Eisenberg, eds.

HIV: Issues with Mental Health and Illness. Binghamton, NY: Haworth Press, 2007.

Angela Brintlinger and Ilya Vinitsky, eds.

Madness and the Mad in Russian Culture. Toronto, Canada: University of Toronto Press, 2007.

Catherine Coleborne and Dolly MacKinnon, eds.

"Madness" in Australia: Histories, Heritage, and the Asylum. St. Lucia, Queensland: University of Queensland Press, 2003.

Erin P. Finley

Fields of Combat: Understanding PTSD Among Veterans of Iraq and Afghanistan. Ithaca, NY: ILR Press, 2011.

Ronald J. Glasser

Broken Bodies/Shattered Minds: A Medical Odyssey from Vietnam to Afghanistan. Palisades, NY: History Publishing Company, 2011.

David Greenberg and Eliezer Witztum	*Sanity and Sanctity: Mental Health Work Among the Ultra-Orthodox in Jerusalem.* New Haven, CT: Yale University Press, 2001.
Marya Hornbacher	*Sane: Mental Illness, Addiction and the 12 Steps.* Center City, MN: Hazelden, 2010.
Yuko Kawanishi	*Mental Health Challenges Facing Contemporary Japanese Society: The "Lonely" People.* Kent, UK: Global Oriental, 2009.
Ronald C. Kessler and T. Bedirhan Ustun	*The WHO World Mental Health Surveys: Global Perspectives on the Epidemiology of Mental Disorders.* New York: Cambridge University Press, 2008.
Roland Littlewood	*Pathologies of the West: An Anthropology of Mental Illness in Europe and America.* Ithaca, NY: Cornell University Press, 2002.
Sana Loue	*"My Nerves Are Bad": Puerto Rican Women Managing Mental Illness and HIV Risk.* Nashville, TN: Vanderbilt University Press, 2011.
Angela McCarthy and Catharine Coleborne, eds.	*Migration, Ethnicity, and Mental Health: International Perspectives, 1840–2010.* New York: Routledge, 2012.
Almerindo E. Ojeda, ed.	*The Trauma of Psychological Torture.* Westport, CT: Praeger, 2008.

Mao-Sheng Ran et al.

Family-Based Mental Health Care in Rural China. Hong Kong: Hong Kong University Press, 2005.

Nancy Scheper-Hughes

Saints, Scholars, and Schizophrenics: Mental Illness in Rural Ireland. Twentieth Anniversary Edition, Updated and Expanded. Berkeley: University of California Press, 2001.

Sam Tsemberis

Housing First Manual: The Pathways Model to End Homelessness for People with Mental Illness and Addiction. Center City, MN: Hazelden, 2010.

Daniel Hack Tuke

The Insane in the United States and Canada. Charleston, SC: Nabu Press, 2010.

Ethan Watters

Crazy Like Us: The Globalization of the American Psyche. New York: Free Press, 2010.

Index

Geographic headings and page numbers in **boldface** refer to viewpoints about that country or region.

A

Abortion, sex-selective, 16–17

Abuses of mentally ill
  health care professionals, 82–83
  "punitive psychiatry," 124, 126, 127–128, 129, 183
  Romania, 85, 86–92
  See also Human rights and rights violations

Access to treatment. *See* Treatment

Accidents, 44, 136, 152

Acute stress disorder, 43

Addiction clinics, 182

Adolescents
  development and alcohol effects, 153
  mental health treatment, Mexico, 218–224
  suicide and alcohol use, 144, 151, 152–157

Affordable housing, 197–198, 202, 203–205

Afghan Red Crescent Society, 21–22

Afghanistan, 20–25, 26–32
  British soldiers' PTSD from war, 26–32, 30*t*
  drug trade, 179–180
  mental health system inadequate to deal with war stresses, 20–25
  population totals, mental health issues, 22, 24
  women's mental health, 24

Aftershocks, earthquakes, 42, 56, 59, 60

Alcohol Action Ireland, 151–157

Alcohol use and abuse
  developing countries, 133, 134, 138–146, 169, 170–171, 173
  Eastern Europe, 178, 179, 180, 181, 182
  effects, 142, 143–144, 152, 181
  harmful drinking patterns, 133, 134, 141, 142–143, 145, 151, 179, 181
  HIV/AIDS patients, 210
  Ireland, 151–157
  moderate use, 134, 143, 145–146
  per-capita consumption data, 140–141, 140*t*
  research, 133, 134–135, 140–146, 152–153, 154–155
  South Africa, 210
  "substance abuse disorder," 136, 142
  women's alcoholism, 16

Alizada, Nowroz Ali, 21

All-Union Society of Psychiatrists and Narcologists, 125, 126

Amankwah, Ama Achiaa, 15

American Correctional Association, 102–103

American Psychological Association, 61, 62

Amnesty International, 107–116

Antiretroviral drugs, 211

Anxiety
  gender differences, 24
  Holocaust survivors and families, 33, 36, 37
  homelessness, 200
  incidence, 135–136
  military members, 28
  trauma-related mental health disorders, 41, 42, 43, 59–60
Arab women, 16, 24
Arap, Larisa, 126, 128, 129
Argentina, 212–217
Asia. *See* China; India; Japan; Singapore; Southeast Asia
Asian Americans, 15
Asylums. *See* Psychiatric hospitals
Auschwitz-Birkenau concentration camp, 35
Australia
  incarceration rates, 99*t*
  psychiatrist-to-population ratios, 191
Avoidance behaviors, 60, 61, 84
Azerbaijan, 180

B

Bagram Theater Internment Facility (Afghanistan), 65
Bangladesh, 173
Basoglu, Metin, 53–62, 67–68, 69
Bauer, Yehuda, 36
Bedar, Asha, 16
Beggars, 21
Belarus, 180
Bell, Vaughan, 124–130
Benjet, C., 218–224
Bereavement, 47–48, 152
Binge drinking, 134, 141, 145, 151, 153, 181
Bipolar disorder, 94, 136
Black, Aaron, 31

Black, June, 31
Blame, post-trauma, 53, 55, 56, 57
Bodibe, Khopotso, 206–211
Body of Principles for the Protection of All Persons Under Any Form of Detention or Imprisonment, 113
Bogopane-Zulu, Hendrietta, 209–211
Borges, G., 218–224
Borsa Castle, Romania, 86–87
Brain
  development, adolescence, 153
  function, HIV and AIDS, 206, 209
Brazil
  domestic violence, 15
  substance use and mental health, 142
Burial customs, Haiti, 47–48

C

Canada, 196–205
  incarceration rates, 99*t*
  mental illness stigmatized, 74
  providing mentally ill with housing can aid recovery, 196–205
Canadian Mental Health Association (Ontario), 196–205
Catani, Claudia, 68–69
Central Asia, 179–180
  See also Afghanistan
Central Intelligence Agency (CIA), 65
Chandra, Vijay, 168–174
Children's mental health
  children of Holocaust victims, 33, 34–39
  education aptitude and access, 137
  fears, 61

Haitian children, 45
teenage development and alcohol effects, 153
violence effects, 22–23
See also Adolescents
Chile, 143–144
China, 117–123
incarceration rates, 99*t*
manufacturing, 118
medicine as state weapon, 118–120
mental health system used to silence dissent, 117–123
political history, 118, 119, 120, 122, 123
population policy and gender preferences, 16–17
Chong, Siow-Ann, 189–195
Coerced confessions, 113–114
Cognitive behavioral therapy, 165, 166
Cognitive effects, post-trauma, 42, 55, 56, 57, 61
Colonial-era drinking habits, 139
Combat Stress (British charity), 29
Communism-to-capitalism transitions, 118, 175, 177–178
Community-based health services
barriers to implementation, 171
housing support, 203
shifts to, from psychiatric hospitals, 76, 89, 168, 169–171
Southeast Asia, needs for shifts to, 168–174
strategies, 172–174
substance abuse treatment, 168, 169–171, 173
trials pointing to efficacy, 138
Community-based housing, 78–79
Community psychology, 48, 178–179, 184–185

Companionship programs, 212–217
Complicated grief, 47–48
Conduct disorder, 220
Confessions, 113–114
Control
feelings of, as therapeutic aid, 46, 49, 50, 60, 61, 202
lack of, as psychological stressor (disasters and accidents), 45, 56, 58–59, 60, 69
lack of, as psychological stressor (torture), 58–59, 63, 68, 69
Convention Against Torture and Other Cruel, Inhuman or Degrading Treatment or Punishment, 102, 104
Cornah, Deborah, 158–167
Corrigan, Patrick W., 72–84
Council of State Governments, 99–100
Counseling
military members, 31–32
possibilities, post-2010 Haiti earthquake, 46–47
post-2011 Japan earthquake, 59–60
smoking cessation, 165, 166
Crime reporting, 80
Criminal justice professionals
incarcerating mentally ill, 94
as power group, 78, 80–81
Culpability, criminal acts, 109, 112–113
Cultural considerations
Eastern Europe, 175, 184–185
gender and mental health, 15, 16–17, 24, 223
Haiti, 46, 47–48
Japan, 62
Southeast Asia, 168, 171–172, 191

Cyclones, 173

Czechoslovakia, 177

D

The Daily Mirror (newspaper), 26–32

Danger beliefs, about mentally ill persons, 74, 75, 80, 83, 192, 204

Dasberg, Haim, 34–35, 37

Death causes, 136, 152, 181, 190

Death penalty
  Amnesty International opposition, 111, 115–116
  Japan, mentally ill criminals, 107–116
  United States, 113

Death rates, asylums, 87, 90

Deegan, P.E., 74

Dementia, 190

Demographic imbalances (gender), 16–17

Depression
  alcohol use links, 142, 144, 145, 153, 155, 156
  community-based treatments, 138
  complicated grief, 47–48
  gender differences, 14–15, 24
  HIV/AIDS and, 208–209, 210
  homelessness, 196, 200
  incidence, 14, 94, 135–136, 190
  mothers, and infant health, 137–138
  within post-traumatic stress disorder, 28, 43
  stereotypes, 75, 82
  tobacco use and, 162–163, 165
  trauma-related mental health disorders, 14–15, 28, 41–42, 60, 64

Developing countries
  access to treatment, 24, 42–43, 169, 171–172, 191, 219–220
  alcohol use/abuse, 133–146, 169, 170–171, 173
  mental health snapshots, 135–138, 174

Diagnoses
  differences by gender, 14
  failures, professionals, 223
  HIV, 209, 210
  incarceration method, 16

Disabilities
  functional, 94, 136, 191–192
  intellectual, 181, 191
  physical, 74–75

Disability-adjusted life years (DALYs), 135, 136

Disaster preparedness, 51

Dissent. *See* Political dissent

Domestic violence
  alcohol use and, 134, 144
  shelters, 200
  war-torn areas, 20, 22–23
  women's mental health, 15

Dopamine, 162, 163

Douki, S., 16

Downs, A., 178

Drivers' licenses, 75

Drug abuse
  Eastern Europe, 175, 178, 179–180, 182, 183
  HIV/AIDS and, 175, 178, 179–180, 183, 210
  Mexico, treatment, 220
  Southeast Asia, community-based care, 168, 169–171, 173
  "substance abuse disorder," 136, 220, 221

Dual diagnosis (mental illness and substance abuse), 176, 179–180, 181, 183, 185–186

E

Earthquakes
 Haiti, 2010, 40, 41–45, 47*t*
 Japan, 2011, 53, 54, 58, 59–62
 nature of trauma, 53, 54–56, 57–60, 61, 62
 timelines, disaster responses, 48–52
 Turkey, 1999, 55
Eastern Europe, 175–186
 Holocaust survivors and families, 34, 35–36
 problems with mental health and substance abuse, 175–186
 See also Romania; Russia
Eating disorders, 16
Ebrahim, Zofeen, 16
Economic system transitions, 118, 175, 177–178
Education
 lower attainment for mentally ill, 192
 Millennium Development Goals, and children, 137
 parental, and treatment rates, 223
 programs within rehabilitation, 76
 as protective factor against illness, 44–45
 public awareness, mental health, 50–51, 81, 146, 171, 173, 186
 substance abuse education, 151, 156–157, 173
Elderly, dementia, 190
Electric shock treatments, 119
Emergency relief, 45–46, 48–49, 62, 173
Emigration, 179

Employment
 beliefs about mentally ill, 77, 79
 companionship programs, 212, 213, 214
 housing challenges, 199, 200
 mentally ill workers, 79–80, 138, 191–192, 195
 prisoners' reentry to society, 99
 psychiatrists' compensation, 193
 self-esteem links, 178
 training for mentally ill, 74, 79, 80, 186, 203
 training needed, professionals, 175, 182, 185, 218
Ethiopia, 144
European Union
 alcohol consumption, 153
 HIV rates, 180
 mental health policies, 90, 184
 suicide rates, 154
 See also Eastern Europe
Executions. *See* Death penalty

F

Fairweather, Clive, 29
Falklands conflict (1982), 28, 29
Falun Gong (Chinese religious group), 117, 121, 122
Families of mentally ill
 abandoning patients, 90
 as caretakers, 136, 183, 184
 homeless people, 200
 military mothers, 26, 29, 31–32
 as power/stigmatizing group, 78, 83–84
 prisoners, 96, 110
 as reformers, 183, 184
 shared anxiety, 33, 34–39
Fatimie, Mohammad Amin, 25

Fear
    of mentally ill persons, 74, 75,
        80, 83, 192, 204
    post-trauma, 42, 53, 56, 57,
        60, 61
Federal benefit programs, US,
    105–106
Federal Bureau of Prisons, 105
Ford v. Wainwright (1986), 113
Forensic psychiatry, 114–115, 127
    Japan, 107, 108, 109
    United States, 113
Foster, John Bellamy, 99t
Freeman, Melvyn, 207–209
Funding and resources, mental
    health programs
    increasing national programs,
        137, 189, 193–194
    underfunded and -resourced
        prison programs, 95, 104–
        105
    underfunded companionship
        programs, 216
    underfunded national pro-
        grams, 82, 181, 182, 184,
        189, 193, 216, 222
    understaffed national pro-
        grams, 136, 174, 191, 193,
        223

G

Gauvain, Tony, 28, 29
Gays, institutionalization, 117,
    119, 121
Gender and mental health
    alcohol use patterns, 133, 134,
        141, 144, 153, 179
    alcoholism, 16
    anxiety, 24
    cultural inequalities, 15, 16–
        17, 24, 223
    Russians' health, 181
    suicide, 15, 24, 154, 179, 181

trauma differences, 14–15, 24
treatment differences, 14, 223
women's challenges/gender
    violence, 14–15, 144
General practitioners, 174, 191,
    193
    See also Health care providers
Generalized anxiety disorder. See
    Anxiety
Genocide, 36–37
    See also Holocaust survivors
Georgia, 180, 184
Germany
    life expectancy comparisons,
        181
    mental illness stigmatized, 74
    political history, 177
"Global Burden of Disease and
    Risk Factors" (report), 145
Global Program Against Stigma
    and Discrimination Because of
    Schizophrenia, 75
Government housing supports,
    204
Government policy makers
    Chinese state medicine, 118–
        120, 123
    developing nations, interest in
        mental health, 137, 170–171,
        193–195
    Eastern Europe, 183
    HIV and AIDS, 211
    as power group, 78, 81–82
    Russian state medicine, 124,
        125, 126, 127–128, 129
    See also Public mental health
        policy
Grassian, Stuart, 66
Grief, complicated, 47–48
Grier, Julie R., 40–52
Group therapy
    not possible, prisons, 98

possibilities, post-2010 Haiti earthquake, 47

Guantánamo Bay (U.S. detention facility) inmates, 64, 65–69

H

Haiti, 40–52

deaths and property damage, 2010 earthquake, 47*t*

needs mental health services in wake of earthquake, 40–52

Halfway houses, 198–199, 201–202, 204

Hamers, F., 178

Health care providers

care as state weapon, China, 118–120

care as state weapon, Russia, 127, 129

corrections facilities, 95, 97–98, 104–105

discrimination against mentally ill, 75, 82, 84, 182

harms to mentally ill, 82–83

mental health as essential component, 170, 171, 174, 191, 193

mental health care, Mexico, 220–221

mental health misunderstood, 192–193

needs, Eastern Europe, 175, 181, 182, 185–186

personal path stories, 120–121

as power group, 78, 82–83

ratios, developed vs. developing nations, 136, 174, 191, 223

Singapore system, 191, 192

smoking bans, 158

training, 175, 182, 218

Health insurance

discrimination against mental health problems, 82, 192

public benefits, 105–106

Singapore national programs, 191, 192

Helplessness. *See* Control

Hepatitis, 180

Heroin, 179–180

Hesketh, Therese, 17

Hifumi, Takezawa, 108

High-risk behaviors, 134, 141, 178, 206, 208, 210

Hirsch, Siegi, 38

HIV/AIDS

China, 121, 122

Eastern Europe, 175, 178, 179–180, 183

effects on brain function, 206, 209

mental health treatment within care, South Africa, 206–211

risk factors, 138, 208–209

Holleman, Hannah, 99*t*

Holocaust survivors, 33–39

Holocaust Trauma: Psychological Effects and Treatment (Kellermann), 34

Homeless people, 200

Afghanistan, 21–22, 23

Canada, 196, 199–200

Haiti, 41, 45

Sweden, 201

Homosexuals, institutionalization, 117, 119, 121

Housing needs

Canada, and aid in health recovery, 196–205

mental illness stigmatization challenges, 78–79, 204

prisoners' reentry to society, 99–100

Sweden, and aid in health recovery, 201
See also Homeless people
Howat, Nicola, 31–32
Human experimentation, 66
Human-made disasters, 54–55, 57
Human rights and rights violations
China, 117–123
developing nations' mentally ill, 137
Eastern European mental facilities, 85–92, 124–130, 181, 182
housing, 197
improvements, Eastern Europe, 183
Japan, mentally ill and death penalty, 107–116
torture, 100
US prisons, 93, 100–106
Human Rights Watch, 93–106
Hungary, 177–178
Hunger, 23, 36, 42, 44
Hurricane Ivan (2004), 55
Hurricane Katrina (2005), 48, 49
Hurricanes, 44–45, 48, 49, 55
Hygiene, hospitals, 85, 87, 88

I

Ilea, Radu, 88
Incarceration policies
global incarceration rates, 99t, 104, 110
Japan's death row, 107, 108–111
US' "Supermax" prisons, 96–98, 101–102, 105
violent vs. nonviolent crime, 93, 104
women's health, 16
See also Prisoners

Independent Psychiatric Association of Russia, 125, 126–127, 130
India
alcohol use and mental health, 141, 142, 143, 144
drug trade, 170
incarceration rates, 99t
Infant health and mortality, 137–138
Injectable drug use, 179–180
Insanity pleas, 109, 112, 113
Insurance. *See* Health insurance
Integrated Regional Information Networks, 20–25
International Association for Women's Mental Health, 14
International Covenant on Civil and Political Rights (ICCPR), 102, 111, 113
International standards and statutes
anti-death penalty, 102, 107, 109, 111, 112, 113
anti-torture, 102, 104
housing, 197
psychiatry, 129
treatment of mentally ill, 100–102, 107, 109, 111, 113–114
International Statistical Classification of Diseases and Related Health Problems (World Health Organization), 142
Intervention methods
Haiti, post-2010 earthquake, 46–47, 49–52
HIV/AIDS care, 207
natural disasters, generally, 53, 55–57, 61
traumatic stress, 56, 57, 60
Iraq war, 2003-2011, 26, 27
Ireland, 151–157
IRIN, 20–25

Isolation
    gender segregation, 24
    social, 73, 83, 84, 182
    solitary confinement, detainment and torture, 65, 66, 67
    solitary confinement, US prisons, 93, 96–97, 101–102, 103, 105
Israel, 72–84
    Holocaust survivors and families, 34–35, 39
    incarceration rates, 99*t*
    mental health funding, 82
    stigma and discrimination against mentally ill, 72–84
"Istanbul Statement on the Use and Effects of Solitary Confinement," 101–102

J

Japan, 53–62, 107–116
    death penalty for mentally ill criminals, 107–116
    incarceration rates, 99*t*, 110
    life expectancy comparisons, 181
    needs to respond to stress caused by earthquake, 53–62
    tsunami, 2011, 58
Job training
    care providers, and needs, 175, 182, 185, 218
    companionship programs, 212, 214–215
    mentally ill, 74, 79, 80, 186, 203
Jonna, R. Jamil, 99*t*
Jönsson, Ann, 201

K

Kalichman, Seth C., 210
Kellermann, Natan, 33, 34–39
Keukens, Rob, 175–186

Krasnov, Valery, 130
Kubota, Keiichiro, 59
Kyrgyzstan, 180, 184

L

Landlords, 78–79
Laos, 170
Latin America, treatment rates, 221–222
Lebanon, 43
"Lessons for Japan's Survivors: The Psychology of Recovery" (article), 54–55, 56–57
Levav, I., 78
Li Hongzhi, 122
Life expectancy, 178, 181
Lindsay, James, 31–32
Ludermir, A.B., 15
Lupo, Simona, 90
Lurie, Mark, 210
Lusted, Marcia Amidon, 58

M

Mamani, Gladys, 214, 216–217
Mao Zedong, 120
McChesney, Robert W., 99*t*
Media
    Chinese policies, 122
    misguided "expert" opinions, on trauma, 54–55, 56–57, 59–60, 61–62
    as power group/perpetuator of stereotypes, 78, 83
Medicaid, 105–106
Medical savings accounts, 191
Medication
    affordability, 172, 182
    forced, dissidents, 126
    given as basic psychiatric care, 137

overmedication and addiction, 85, 91
smoking cessation, 165, 166
super-maximum security prisons, 98
See also Self-medication
Medina-Mora, M.E., 218–224
Mental asylums. *See* Psychiatric hospitals
Mental health reforms
developing nations, 137
Eastern Europe/Russia, 126, 183–184
Israel, 76
needed, Mexico, 221–223
recommendations, US, 102–106
Singapore, 189, 193–195
Mental state assessments, 114–115
Mentally Ill Offender Treatment and Crime Reduction Act (2004), 104
Mexico, 218–224
Military members
British soldiers, Afghanistan war trauma, 26–32, 30*t*
mental health statistics, 27–28, 29, 30*t*
suicide, 26, 28, 31
Military training, 65
Millennium Development Goals (United Nations), 137
Ministry of Public Health (Afghanistan), 22, 25
Moldova, 180, 184
Moscow to the End of the Line (Yerofeyev), 179
Mudslides, 44–45
Myanmar, 170, 173

N

Nadimee, Musadiq, 22
National Alliance on Mental Illness, 15

National Commission on Correctional Health Care, 102–103
National Israeli Center for Psychological Support of Survivors of the Holocaust and the Second Generation, 34–35
Natural disasters
Asian 2004 tsunami, 173
Haiti 2010 earthquake, 40, 41–52
Haitian environment, 44–45
Japan 2011 earthquake, 53, 54, 58, 59–62
nature of trauma, 53, 54–60, 61, 62
preparedness, 51
timelines, post-disaster care, 48–52
See also Human-made disasters
Nicotine, 162, 163–164, 165, 166
Nonconformity, 120
Nongovernmental organizations, 22, 109, 119, 184, 191
Novinka, Andrei, 128

O

Obama, Barack, 65
One child policy, China, 16–17
Ontario, Canada, 196–205
Ontario Disability Support Program, 204
Opium, 170
Orozco, R., 218–224
Orphans, 39, 45
Overmedication, 85, 91
Ownby, David, 122

P

Pakistan, 16, 170
"Passive euthanasia," 88, 90
Patel, Vikram, 133–150

Peng, Tina, 15

Physical vs. psychological torture, 63, 64–69

Physicians, 174, 191, 193
  See also Health care providers

Physicians for Human Rights, 64, 65

Poland, 177–178

Political dissent
  Chinese mental health system utilized to silence, 117–123
  Russian mental health system utilized to silence, 124–130

Political prisoners, 119, 126, 128

Popova, Olga, 128

Population policies, national, 16–17

Post-traumatic stress disorder (PTSD)
  disaster environments, 41, 42, 43, 44, 55, 60
  gender, 14, 24
  included mental health conditions, 28, 43
  torture victims, 64, 67–69
  war (military members), 26–32, 30*t*
  war zones (locals), 22, 24, 37
  See also Trauma causes of mental illness

Postcolonial drinking habits, 139

Poverty
  Afghanistan, and mental health system, 20, 21–22, 23
  Eastern Europe, and mental health, 178
  employment to avoid, 79
  Haiti, and 2010 earthquake, 42–43, 44–45, 52
  mental health treatment's influence over, 138
  mental illness links, 178, 192, 200, 204

Ontario, and housing needs, 197, 199, 200, 202, 204

Powell, Devin, 63–69

Powell, Lewis, 113

Power groups, in society, 77–79, 80–83

Pre-exposure factors, 37–38, 44–45

Precolonial drinking habits, 138–139

Pregnancy, 137

Préval, René, 47*t*

Prison Litigation Reform Act (1996), 103–104

Prison reform, 102–106

Prisoners
  death penalty, Japanese mentally ill, 107–116
  Guantánamo Bay (U.S. detention facility) inmates, 64, 65–69
  health risks of prison, 85, 87, 88, 178, 180
  incarceration rates by country, 99*t*, 104
  lack of public support for treatment, 95
  mental illness rates vs. whole population, 94
  mentally ill face inhumane conditions, US, 93–106
  See also Political dissent

Prisoners of war, 66, 67–68

Privates, military, 27, 28, 30*t*

Proia, Cristina, 213, 214, 215–216

Prostitution, 178, 180

Protective factors against mental illness, 178
  early interventions, 56
  education, 44, 45
  feelings of control, 46, 49, 50, 60, 61, 202
  social networks, 45, 49, 51, 178–179

Psychiatric hospitals
child psychiatry, 223
Chinese, state-run, 123
companionship programs as cost-effective alternative, 212, 213–214, 216
housing as cost-effective alternative, 196, 202, 204
orders of admission, criminal justice system, 80–81
Romania, brutal conditions, 85, 86–92
Russian, state-run, 124, 125, 181
shifts to community-based facilities, 76, 89, 168, 169–171
smoking bans, and effects, 158, 159–167
social isolation, 182
Psychiatry, 192–193
See also Health care providers; "Punitive psychiatry"
Psycho-education programs, 50–51
Psychological torture, 63, 64–69, 93, 101
Psychotic disorders
community-based treatments, 138
drug therapies, 137
incidence, 136
Public health
adolescent mental health, Mexico, 223–224
companionship programs, 216
falling standards and levels, Eastern Europe, 175, 178, 180, 182
population-based model, 194
See also Alcohol use and abuse; Health care providers; Mental health reforms
Public mental health policy
developing in developing nations, 137, 193–195

needs, Eastern Europe, 181, 182
needs, Haiti, 51
needs, Japan, 62
Puerto Rico, 221
"Punitive psychiatry," 124, 126, 127–128, 129, 183

Q

Qigong, 122
Quitting smoking, 159, 160, 162–163, 164–166

R

Radiation leakage, 57
Rates of mentally ill populations
adults, global, 135–136, 190
at-risk populations, 180
gender differences, 14, 24, 144
HIV-positive individuals, 207–208
increase trends, 181, 190, 207–208
prisoners, 94
traumatized populations, 43, 49–50
Red Crescent Society, 21–22
Reentry to society
mentally ill, from facilities, 182, 216
prisoners, 98–100, 105–106
Reforms. *See* Mental health reforms
Refugees, 43, 45
Religious communities
Haiti, 47, 48, 50
state opposition and punitive psychiatry, 117, 121, 122, 127
traditional medicine links, 171–172, 191
Remaeus, Annika, 201

Rental housing and supports, 197, 198–199, 202, 203, 204–205

Research
alcohol use and mental health, 133, 134–135, 140–146, 152–153, 154–155
clinical and community psychology, 48
effects of torture, 63, 64, 66–69
mental health, Singapore, 193
mental illness and HIV, 208–209
nicotine, 163–164
stigmatization attitudes, 76–77
trauma-related mental illness, 44, 48, 54–55, 57–58, 61

Resources. *See* Funding and resources, mental health programs

Rights to fair trial, 113–114

Roe, David, 72–84

Romania, 85–92
mental health care system, 89, 176
mentally ill treated with brutality and contempt, 85–92
political history, 90
See also Eastern Europe

Roy Walmsley's International Centre for Prison Studies, 99*t*

Russia, 124–130
HIV rates, 180
incarceration rates, 99*t*
mental health system may be used to silence dissent, 124–130
poor population health and habits, 181
See also Eastern Europe

Rwanda, 99*t*

S

Salvage, Jane, 175–186

Savenko, Yuri, 124–130

Schizophrenia
community-based treatments, 138
incidence, 94, 136
prisoners, 97, 109
smoking habits, 163, 165
social distance by outsiders, 82

Schmidt-Michel, Paul-Otto, 87–88, 90, 91

School-based treatments, 220, 221, 224

Secondary traumas, 44, 56, 59, 60

Segregation by gender, 24

Seiha, Fujima, 108

Self-harm
alcohol-related, 153, 155, 156
self-immolation, 86
self-mutilation, 96, 97

Self-help
groups, 183, 184
mental health interventions, 56
self-empowerment, 83–84

Self-medication
alcohol use, 156, 210
military members, 28
smoking, 163–164

Self-stigmatization, 78, 83, 84

Sensory deprivation, 65, 68

September 11, 2001 terrorist attacks, 48

Sex-selective abortion, 16–17

Sex work, 178, 180

Sexism, 14–15, 16–17

Sexual humiliation, 65

Shelters, 200

Shinji, Mukai, 108

Siegel-Itzkovich, Judy, 33–39

Singapore, 189–195

Skaine, Rosemarie, 24

Sleep deprivation, 65

Sleep problems, 31, 59, 60, 137

Smoking ban, United Kingdom, 158–167

Smoking cessation, 159, 160, 162–163, 164–166

Smoking habits, 158, 159, 161–162, 164*t*, 181

Social cohesion, 178–179, 184–185

Social distance

    prisoners, 96, 97, 99–100

    result of stigmatization, 84, 181

    societal systems of isolation, 77–78, 81–82, 182

Social inclusion

    companionship programs, 212–217

    housing successes, 203

    mental health treatment, 73, 74, 76

Social networks

    employment, 79

    HIV patients' needs, 209

    post-trauma influences, 45

    utilized in therapies, 47, 49, 51, 74

Social norms, 46

Social Security Disability Insurance, 79, 105–106

Solitary confinement

    calls for rare use/elimination, 101–102, 105

    detainment and torture, 65, 66, 67

    US prisons, 93, 96–97, 101–102, 103, 105

South Africa, 206–211

Southeast Asia, 168–174

    See also Singapore

Soviet Union, 124, 125–126, 127, 176, 177

    See also Eastern Europe; Russia

Standard Minimum Rules for the Treatment of Prisoners, 113

Stereotypes

    beliefs about mentally ill, 73, 74, 75, 76–77, 79, 80, 192, 214–215

    beliefs of mental health professionals, 75, 82, 84, 182

    reducing, 81, 214–215

    women, and barriers to treatment, 16

    See also Stigma of mental illness

Stigma of alcohol and drug abuse, 146, 182

Stigma of HIV/AIDS, 180, 210

Stigma of mental illness, 192

    Asian-American communities, 15

    Asian nations, 168, 171, 189, 192–193

    China, 118–119, 120, 123

    Germany, 74

    government-encouraged, 123, 184

    Haiti, 46, 50

    history, 73

    housing challenges, 78–79, 204

    Israel, 72, 76–84

    Mexico, 218, 222–223

    plans and programs to remove, 50, 72, 75, 76, 81, 84, 186, 193

    Romania, enabling brutal conditions, 85, 86, 89

    self-stigmatization, 78, 83, 84

    treatment despite, 29

    United States, 15, 74

    worldwide, 72, 73–76, 137

Stigma of non-traditional sexuality, 121

Stigma of poverty, 178, 204

Struch, N., 76–77

Stuart, H., 83

Subcommittee on Human Rights and the Law, US Congress, 103

Substance abuse. *See* Alcohol use and abuse; Drug abuse; Dual diagnosis (mental illness and substance abuse)

Suicide
    alcohol consumption and abuse, 133, 134, 142, 143–144, 151–157, 179, 181
    Arab women, 16, 24
    Asian Americans, 15
    Eastern Europeans, 178, 181
    gender differences, 15, 24, 154, 179, 181
    mental patients, 86, 96
    prisoners, 96, 97
    Singapore, 190
    soldiers, 26, 28, 31
    stigmatization of mental illness, 83
    workers, 118, 142

"Supermax" prisons, 96–98, 101–102, 105

Superstition, 171–172

Supplemental Security Income, 79, 105–106

"Supportive" and "supported" housing, 198–199, 201–202, 204

Supreme Court (United States), 113

Sweden, 201

Switzerland, 75

T

Tajikistan, 180

Tal, Amir, 72–84

Taliban, 24

Tamms Correctional Center (Illinois), 96–97

Tataru, Nicoleta, 89

Teenage development, 153

Thailand, 170

Therapies. *See* Treatment

Thom, Rita, 209

Timelines, disaster response, 48–52

Torture
    human rights tenets, 100
    long-term effects on the mind, 63–69, 93, 101
    survivors, earthquake survivor comparisons, 55, 58–59
    US prison conditions as, 93, 101, 102

Traditional medicine, 171–172, 191

Traffic accidents, 44, 136, 152

Training. *See* Job training; Military training

Tranquilizers, 91

Transitional housing, 198–199, 201–202, 204

Trauma causes of mental illness, 42–44
    cognitive effects, post-trauma, 42, 55, 56, 57, 61
    domestic violence, 15, 20, 22–23
    gender violence, 14, 15
    grief, 47–48
    Holocaust, 33–39
    misconceptions, 54–56, 61–62
    natural disasters, 40, 41–46, 48, 49, 51–52, 53–62
    secondary traumas, 44, 56, 59, 60
    society-wide traumas, 41–42, 43, 46, 48, 51–52, 55–57
    torture, 55, 58–59, 63–69, 93, 101
    wars, 20–25, 26–32

Treatment

access, general health services, 45–46, 49, 136–137

access differences, gender, 14

access limitations, geographic (Afghanistan), 20, 21–22, 23, 24, 25

access limitations, geographic (developing countries), 133, 136, 171–172, 174, 219–220, 223–224

access limitations, geographic (Haiti), 40, 41–43, 45–46, 48–49, 51–52

access limitations, political (China), 118–120, 123

access limitations, political (Russia), 124

adolescents, Mexico, 218–224

companionship programs, 212–217

distance and cost issues, 172, 182, 192, 218, 224

economic outcomes, 138

in HIV/AIDS care, South Africa, 206–211

improving, Singapore, 189–195

mental health access failures, national health systems, 82, 89, 136, 174, 181, 183, 192, 219–220, 223–224

military members, seeking, 29, 31–32

post-disaster care, 48–52, 55–57, 61

prisoners face poor conditions, 93, 95, 97–98, 103–104

psychotherapy, trauma victims, 28, 69

rehabilitation services, 74, 76, 94–95

stigmas as barrier, 73–74, 77–80, 83, 89, 218, 222–223

willingness to seek, by gender, 16

See also Community-based health services; Counseling; Funding and resources, mental health programs; Health care providers; Intervention methods; Medication; Psychiatric hospitals

Triple diagnosis (mental illness, substance abuse, and HIV/AIDS), 176, 180, 183

Troop training, 65

Tsemberis, Sam, 201

Tsunamis, 58, 173

Tsutomu, Miyazaki, 108–109

U

UK Mental Health Foundation, 154–155

Ukraine, 180, 184

Unemployment, 79–80, 138, 178, 199

United Kingdom, 26–32, 158–167

alcohol use and abuse, 155–156

incarceration rates, 99t

mental illness stigmatized, 75

psychiatrist-to-population ratios, 191

smoking ban raises issues for mental health workers and patients, 158–167

smoking habits, 158, 159, 161–162, 164t

soldiers' post-Afghanistan PTSD, 26–32

United Nations

Committee Against Torture, 102, 104

Economic and Social Council, 111

Human Rights Committee, 100, 102, 111, 114

Millennium Development Goals, 137

Office for the Coordination of Humanitarian Affairs, 20
UNICEF, 45
United States, 63–69, 93–106
Asian American suicides, 15
capital cases and death penalty, 113
incarceration rates, 99*t*, 104
mental health funding, 82
mental illness stigmatized, 74
mentally ill prisoners face inhumane conditions, 93–106
psychiatrist-to-population ratios, 191
Supreme Court cases, 113
torture, 63–69
United States Congress
prison reform recommendations, 102–106
Subcommittee on Human Rights and the Law, 103

V

Valente, Marcela, 212–217
Veterans
government care and support, 26
suicide, 26
See also Military members
Violence against women, and mental health, 14, 15, 144
Vodou, 47

W

Wainwright, Ford v. (1986), 113
Wang, P.S., 218–224
Waterboarding, 65

Wiedemann, Erich, 85–92
Women's rights
Afghanistan, 24
Pakistan, 16
World Congress on Women's Mental Health, 14
World Health Organization (WHO)
Eastern European action, 183–184
gender and mental health, 14
"Mental Health Atlas," 136
national supports of mental health, 193
publications, alcohol and mental health, 142, 154–155
Southeast Asia regional office mission, 169, 170–171
World Mental Health Survey Initiative, 219–220
World Health Surveys, 140
World Prison Population List, 99*t*
World Psychiatric Association, 75, 125–126, 130

X

Xu Lindong, 119

Y

Yanhai, Wan, 117–123
Yerofeyev, Venedict, 179
Yugoslavia, 177

Z

Zhou Yi Juan, 122–123
Zhu, Wei-Xing, 17